Lad duf

D1546359

WAR AND PEACE
IN THE SUDAN

WORLD REALITIES

War and Peace in the Sudan 1955-1972

Cecil Eprile

DAVID & CHARLES
NEWTON ABBOT   LONDON

Set in 11 on 13 Baskerville and printed in
Great Britain by W J Holman Limited
for David & Charles (Holdings) Limited
South Devon House Newton Abbot Devon

Contents

Contents

Introduction

The long war in the Sudan, which began in 1955, went on intermittently until the cease-fire of March 1972. It was regarded by many Southerners as basically a clash between a Northern Arab culture and a Southern Negroid culture. (The terms 'Arab' and 'Negroid' are ethnically not strictly accurate, but I use them for convenience in communication.) The war was followed by a period of transition. The cessation of hostilities came only after many, many thousands of lives had been lost in the Southern Sudan. Many Southerners felt it was a pity that the Organisation of African Unity, the World Council of Churches and (by no means least) the Emperor of Ethiopia, all of whom played important and creditable parts in bringing about a settlement, could not have influenced the situation earlier. Sympathisers with the South have argued that the harsh struggle, which caused so much suffering, so much wastage and so much dislocation, was regarded as an internal matter for the Sudan—an attitude which for many years created a sense of frustration and helplessness among many Southerners. Northerners, on the other hand, say that outside interference made it difficult for the two sides to become reconciled earlier.

The decision to agree to a settlement required a degree of flexibility, vision and courage on both sides. Each side had to make concessions beyond what had previously been regarded as desirable or even acceptable. Well-wishers saw the settlement as a victory for humanity. I was personally in close touch with some of the negotiators on both sides and I am satisfied that they were well aware that such a victory would not be an

7

easy one. The mistrusts that had built up between North and South over a great many years—and which existed long before the revolt of 1955 that sparked off the war—could not be obliterated by a few strokes of the pen. There were too many memories in the South of previous peace negotiations which ended in failure; of broken promises and of dishonoured guarantees. It came as a surprise to outside observers to see in the first year after the agreement at Addis Ababa how little rancour appeared to remain. Some Sudanese say this is the Sudanese way. To me as to many others the progress on the human side was astonishing.

For the negotiators on both sides a period of heavy responsibility lay ahead. There were bound to be interests both inside and outside the country which, either through conviction or from other motivations, would denigrate the agreement as a sell-out, a surrender, a blunder or act of weakness, foolishness or folly. And these elements soon began to manifest their suspicions, fears and hostility. President Nimery, a bluff, energetic soldier, little known until, at the age of 39, he was swept to power by a military coup in May 1969, was one of the two key figures in the ratification of the agreement. His keen awareness of the difficulties in the path of peace in a unified Sudan was shown in the address he made to a rally at Omdurman (3 March 1972) when he admitted shortcomings towards the South not only on the part of previous governments but also during his own regime.

In the past two years, he said, his government had met many obstacles. Now, in the past four months, they had been racing to make up for lost time. He called for patience and warned that there would be people who would try to trap the government into breaking the cease-fire agreement. The greatest troublemakers were likely to be those who had lost power at the time of the 1969 revolution, and were jealous that the revolutionaries had since achieved what they had failed to do in two decades.

'The coming stage,' the President added, 'will be more difficult than the one through which we have passed. We must exert more effort to achieve economic and social development.'

In some ways this seemed to be one of the most perceptive speeches ever made by a Sudanese Head of State; and although the pages of Sudanese history are filled with eloquent declarations that have turned out to be meaningless, I personally consider this particular address by President Nimery to be of notable significance.

Some of the stories I shall tell in this book—of cruelties, even atrocities, of political intrigues and Big Power cynicism, will not make pretty reading. I write about these things not in order to reopen old wounds but because they are part of the story of a bitter war that was followed by encouraging progress towards unity and peace. The brutality of the past made the humanities of the present all the more noteworthy.

The Southerners have a long list of grievances over their treatment at Northern hands—ranging from allegations of traditional attitudes of contempt and master–servant relationship to charges of massacres; and before there could be a settled, peaceful, unified Sudan these resentments had to be openly and freely discussed inside the Sudan. The Northerners, too, have legitimate interests and understandable ambitions and affinities; and I shall try to examine both the Southern and Northern viewpoints as objectively as possible. To put the highly complex problems of the Sudan into perspective, a number of points are worth bearing in mind.

Foreign observers, some of whom were emotionally involved but many of whom were professional people of experience and integrity, agreed that the death toll in the Southern Sudan far exceeded anything admitted by any Khartoum government source—and that the great majority of the victims were not the Southern guerrillas but civilians.

It was unhelpful and counter-productive to talk of genocide.

It has been argued that at certain times in the history of independent Sudan there have been deliberate attempts to destroy the educated Southern elite. But since the May 1969 revolution, the declared policy of the government has been in the contrary direction.

Although there were some material developments in the Sudan during the military reign of General Abboud (1958–1964), the regime's policy of trying to end the Southern revolt by force was responsible for one of the most shameful chapters of the Sudan's history.

Aside from killings and tortures, one of the worst things that happened in the South was the closing down of all schools in 1964–5. The Revolutionary Government of General Nimery made big efforts to speed up educational progress in the South, but government sources admitted that up till 1972 the work of restoration had been disappointingly slow and much remained to be done.

The obstruction of the work of Christian missionaries during the Abboud regime was seen to be against Southern interests, and the expulsion of all foreign missionaries by 1964 may be viewed as high-handed and unreasonable. Government charges that missionaries incited Southerners against the Northerners appeared on the whole to be unfounded or exaggerated.

The extent of Soviet participation in the war against the South from the beginning of 1970 up to the abortive coup of July 1971 was evidently greater than either Khartoum or Moscow admitted. But continued Russian encouragement for communist elements which tried to overthrow the Nimery regime led to changes in Sudan's relations with the Soviet Union and efforts to free the Sudan from Soviet influence and improve relations with the West.

After the June Declaration (9 June 1969) offering regional autonomy to the South, the Nimery government did more than any previous government to put Southerners into positions of responsibility. One test of the government's sincerity was the extent to which, after the war, it enabled former enemy Southerners to be placed in positions of power.

The big issue following the March 1972 agreement was whether the forces of moderation and reconciliation on both sides could prevail. Only if and when peace became a way of life in a unified Sudan could the energies of both areas be freed to develop the country in a meaningful way. What the Sudan needed desperately was a settling-in period and stable government. So long as suspicions remained—and rivalries to feed on them—there would be uncertainties. The encouraging fact was that a start had been made towards peace, and that in the first year of the peace human relations between Northerner and Southerner continued to improve.

CHAPTER ONE

The Sixteen Years' War

This does not pretend to be a definitive history of the conflict in Southern Sudan. It sets out, rather, to give some guidelines to a great human tragedy in a large area which is still relatively unknown and little understood by the outside world. When I visited the Sudan in December 1971, government spokesmen told me that they did not care what I wrote about their country so long as I told the facts. I hope they meant this.

Fighting broke out in the second half of 1955, turned into organised guerrilla warfare in 1963 and came to a halt when the Nimery government ordered a cease-fire after peace talks in Addis Ababa in February 1972. The sixteen-year war has more than once been described as the Soviets' Vietnam and compared with the war in Biafra, the violence in East Pakistan and the Indian wars in America. Comparisons tend to be misleading, but these do convey a sense of the extent of the suffering involved.

Successive Sudanese governments with their power base in the North denied and resented allegations that the war was a racial conflict in which Northern Arab troops oppressed African Southerners. Indeed, by 1971, government spokesmen were claiming that the army in the South had a non-Arab majority, including not only crack black troops from the Nuba mountains and elsewhere but also about 3,000 Southerners.[1] To the Southerners in the bush, however, the troops who came down from the North to attack them looked like Arabs, spoke like Arabs, acted like Arabs and were clearly Arab in all their ways—irrespective of the ethnic niceties of the matter. And

any Southerners who supported them were accused of collab-
orating with the Arab enemy.

The government of General Nimery, which came to power
in a military coup in May 1969, was well aware of what had
happened since the Sudan became independent in 1956 to
make Southerners—and particularly those who had fled to the
bush or into neighbouring countries as refugees—regard
Northerners as their enemies. In addition to publicising
Nimery's 'New Deal' for the South—based on a recognition
that there are differences between the North and South—
government publications after May 1969 made a point of
emphasising the mistakes and misdeeds of previous governments.

In a series entitled, *A Revolution in Action*, the government, through its Ministry for Southern Affairs, condemned
its predecessors as reactionaries who had done nothing in the
fourteen years since independence to alleviate the fears and
suspicions which the Southern problem had aroused. One of
these documents was the text of a speech made by a leading
politician in February 1970 in which, apart from blaming the
military regime of General Ibrahim Abboud for bringing
relations between the North and South to an all-time low
between 1958 and 1964, he openly admitted that government
forces (or, to use his words, 'agents') had so terrorised people
in many remote areas of Southern Sudan that they had fled
into exile or resorted to armed rebellion. He also disclosed
that there had been attempts between 1966 and 1968 to intro-
duce an Islamic constitution for the whole of the Sudan which
would have legalised discrimination on religious and cultural
grounds.[2]

Even before the calculated candour of these publications
there had from time to time been men in the North who, for
one reason or another, found themselves compelled to stand
up and admit that Southerners had suffered wrongs at the
hands of Northerners. Sometimes it took considerable courage
to say this. One of those to speak out was Mohamed Omer
Beshir, a leading Sudanese thinker who became Principal and

Deputy Vice-Chancellor of Khartoum University in late 1971. As early as 1968, he said that, while he believed that many atrocities in the South were the work of the guerrillas on their own people, he also believed that the army had been killing innocent people and, by its repressive behaviour during the Abboud regime, had driven thousands of Southerners out of the Sudan into Uganda, Kenya, Ethiopia and the Central African Republic.[3]

When it started to show serious intentions of negotiating with the Southern Resistance to end the war, the very centre of government revealed a willingness to face up to the realities of the continued divisions between North and South. In December 1971 the Minister of Information was to be found admitting that he was not surprised that some of the Southerners did not trust the Khartoum government. They had, after all, been cheated for fifteen years.[4] Even the President, in a somewhat unusual display of sympathy for guerrillas from a head of state, said the Southern rebels were victims of the policies of deceit practised by his predecessors.[5]

The divisions and the suspicions ran deep. Southerners had long memories of being patronised, exploited and mistreated by Northern traders, civil servants and troops. One of the original causes of the war was a Southern belief that the Northern Arabs regarded and treated Southern Africans as slaves. Justifiably or not, many Southerners felt that the Northerners had *always* been enemies, oppressors and exploiters. The roots of this belief were embedded in history. The South's earlier memories of Arabs were that they were among those who had come as slavers.

The history of the Sudan dates back thousands of years. Although no internal records exist of the early history of the Sudanese people, successive kingdoms along the Nile had sufficient contact with the major civilisations of the Mediterranean world to enable historians to trace a more or less continuous history of much of Northern Sudan. The South, however, remains a misty, mysterious region known virtually only in myth. There were few contacts between the Southern

Sudan and the outside world until 1839 when an expedition from Egypt to explore the source of the Nile penetrated the Sudd (the vast papyrus swamp which to this day hampers navigation between North and South Sudan). The expedition was led by Salim, a Turkish naval captain and it opened for the first time a route from the North into the heart of Central Africa. It also opened the road to the slave traders; and their continued raids on the South—in spite of efforts by the Egyptian government to abolish slavery during the period of Turco–Egyptian rule known as the *Turkiya* which ran from 1820 to 1884—led the Southern tribes, understandably, to regard all those engaged in slavery, whether Egyptians or Northern Sudanese, with intense hostility.[6]

Southerners in modern times were to say that the memory of the Northern slavers had been kept alive to this day because the Northerners continued to treat the Southerners as though they were slaves and had ruled the South since independence like colonialists. Many Northerners, finding this version distasteful and untrue, blamed the missionaries for keeping hostility alive by exploiting the theme of the Northern slavers right up to the time when all foreign Christian missionaries—Catholic and Protestant alike—were expelled from the Southern Sudan by an edict in 1964. (The case for and against the missionaries will be discussed in a later chapter.) A Khartoum government publication maintained that the slave trade in the Southern provinces of Equatoria and Bahr El Ghazal was a result of Turco–Egyptian and European penetration of those regions. The Northern Sudanese were said to have been the assistants and successors of alien traders and not the initiators.[7] The North could produce historical evidence that far from the Arabs being the only slavers to exploit the Southerners, Europeans played no less notorious a role. Even some Southern tribes were involved—for instance, the Nyangulgule of the Raga district.[8] One Southern slaver was said to have dealt in slaves by the thousands.[9] Whether the myth of the rapacious traders was indeed a myth, as some authorities suggest,[10] the force of Southern feeling on the matter was a reality. Indeed,

Southern bitterness persisted into the 1970s and Southern leaders have recorded their historic feelings about the Arabs.[11] As one of them put it: 'The Arab role during the slave trade did earn them hostility in Africa. And although the European colonisation brought slavery to an end, feelings of hatred against the Arabs are still manifest in many parts of Africa today, as they are against the Europeans who took slaves across the Atlantic. This is not to preach racialism. But it should be pointed out that the policies and treatment of the Africans of South Sudan by the Arab-dominated government in Khartoum is similar to that during the slave period.'[12] In spite of the undoubted propaganda motivation of such declarations, at the time, they did underline how much goodwill, patience, determination and readiness to start afresh both Northern and Southern leaders would have to manifest in the future if a new and better era in relationships were to be maintained.

To what extent did British policy under the so-called Anglo–Egyptian Condominium (1899–1956) work towards developing the gulf between North and South which made conflict inevitable? Some historians[13] see the British era as a relatively happy chapter for the Southerners and British intentions towards them as honest and humane. At the same time, they admit that British policy at the time was not consistent or far-sighted. Northern and Southern Sudanese alike seemed to have little doubt that the British decision in 1902 to treat the three Southern provinces (known today as Equatoria, Bahr el Ghazal and Upper Nile) separately from Northern Sudan was *designed* to isolate the North from the South. It seemed to them that Britain deliberately slowed down the development of the southern part of the country while allowing things in the North to take their natural course.[14]

As evidence of this, Northerners quoted the Closed Districts Order of 1922 and the Southern Policy of 1930[15] which, taken together, virtually closed the South to Northern traders. In Northern eyes this was the cutting of an artery. In the view of one distinguished Northerner,[16] British policy saddled the independent Sudan with its most intractable problem when it

B

created a form of local patriotism in the South which, though
not acceptable to everyone living there, sought to speak in the
name of the whole region. It was this local patriotism which,
in its more extreme form, had sought the establishment by
violence of a separate Southern state.

On the British side it was argued that the Southern Policy
was designed not to retard, but to protect, the South. Confidential documents from high British officials in the Sudan,
covering the period 1930 to 1946 (which are in the government archives in Khartoum and purported copies of which
came into my possession) can be interpreted as supporting this
contention. They could, on the other hand, also be used to
support allegations that British policy was carried to absurd
lengths (when, for instance, it substituted biblical names and
British shorts for Arab names and dress[17]) or allegations that
the British government dragged its feet on Southern development. A British observer who had been in close touch with
British policy-making in the Sudan told me (in London in
1971) that there had been little or no organisation in the
South, which was divided by tribal rivalries. According to
him, the use of English was encouraged by the departing Raj
because the British feared that the use of Arabic in the South
would strengthen the sophisticated North against the vulner-
able Southerners. The British had thought there would be
time for the South to build up some kind of administrative
structure of its own.

As it turned out, time was running out too fast for them. In
1946 the Southern Policy was reversed in a declaration which,
while acknowledging the fact that the peoples of the Southern
Sudan were distinctly African and Negroid, also stated that
they were inextricably bound, both geographically and economically, to the Middle Eastern and Arabicised Northern
Sudanese as far as future development was concerned. The
new policy would therefore be to ensure that they were equipped to stand up for themselves as social and economic equals
of the Northerners.[18] The new policy was an early herald of
Sudanese independence and was based on a British recognition

that, with British withdrawal from the Sudan now only a matter of time, the South could not be left to its own devices cut off from the North.

There were many reasons for this new decision. There was Britain's realisation that, in the post-World War II world, colonialism was on the way out. There was the question of repaying the Sudan for the part it had played in World War II (the Sudanese Defence Force, guarding some 1,200 miles of frontier with only 4,500 men, held off many times that number of Italian troops; and later some units from the North served with the British Eighth Army in North Africa). Above all, Britain, with its vast interests in the Suez Canal zone, was anxious to placate an Egypt all too conscious—and resentful—of the fact that it had been a very junior partner in the Anglo–Egyptian Condominium. And just as Britain had used the waters of the Nile as a threat against Egypt in the *Allenby Ultimatum* of 1922 (see chapter 9), so the Egyptians used Suez as a weapon against Britain. Concession followed concession until Egypt, which had become a sovereign power in 1936 and was claiming the whole Sudan as its southern province, felt in a sufficiently strong position to proclaim King Farouk King of Sudan in 1951. In 1952 Farouk was forced to abdicate, and the new Egyptian republic decided to support independence for the Sudan.

Meanwhile Southern intellectuals, who had criticised the British for doing far too little for the Sudan's economic, social and educational development, condemned the reversal of the Southern Policy as a sell-out to the Arabs. Khartoum claimed at the time that the Southerners were fully consulted by the North on the 'one-Sudan' policy and that Southern representatives agreed to this policy at a conference held in 1947 at Juba (the principal town of Southern Sudan). But the educated, articulate minority in the South—whom the Northerners tended to regard as agitators—claimed that their delegates at Juba had been bribed, blackmailed and intimidated into saying 'Yes'. The North, they insisted, broke its promise to give serious consideration to the Southern demand for a federation for the Sudan; and other promised safeguards were never put into force.

The Sudan was granted self-government in 1953 and full independence three years later. The Southern view was that the South was no more ready for one-Sudan independence in 1956 than for 'Sudanisation' in 1954 which, to the Southerners' intense disappointment and resentment, gave them only 6 out of 800 senior government posts to replace British officials. The reason was the backwardness and inexperience of Southerners but it didn't make the decision any more palatable.[19]

Although there had been earlier political activity (much of it underground) in the North—which culminated in an army mutiny in Khartoum in 1924—the Northern Sudanese did not organise themselves on any nation-wide political basis until after 1936. The activity came mainly from people with secondary education (the 'graduates') who in 1938 formed the Graduates' General Congress. Within five years Congress split and out of this split were born the North's two main political parties—the pro-Egyptian National Unionist Party (NUP) and the UMMA (Independent) Party.[20] In 1951 a Southern Sudanese political movement was inaugurated. In 1953 Britain ratified an agreement between the Northern political parties and Egypt concerning future independence; and after Southerners had been excluded from the negotiations on the ground that they had no political party, the Southern movement was officially registered as the Southern Party. In 1954 it changed its name to the Liberal Party. In some Southern eyes this party was to remain the sole representative of Southern aspirations and hopes until all political parties were dissolved in 1958.[21] Southerners took part in elections in October 1953 for the Sudan's first Parliament. The pro-Egyptian NUP won the elections and the party's chairman, Ismail el Azhari, became the Sudan's first Prime Minister. Out of a total of 97 seats the South got 22 and the Southern Party won 16 of them.

In 1955 a series of events occurred which culminated in a large-scale army revolt in the South and which were to trigger off an era of violence there. (The events leading up to and flowing from the mutiny of the Southern Corps are discussed in chapter 3.) Southern accounts of events since independence in 1956 present an almost unvarying picture of alleged repression. Meanwhile a UMMA government had been formed on 7 July 1956 under the premiership of Abdul Bey Khalil, in coalition with the People's Democratic Party (PDP) and the Liberals. Under the pressure of increasing internal difficulties, Mr Khalil, in November 1958, invited the army under General Ibrahim Abboud to take over the government. Relationships between North and South went from bad to worse.

In December 1960, an alleged plot to carry out mass arrests of Southern politicians on Christmas Eve was discovered and a group of them fled from the country to set up an organisation in exile. In 1963 freedom fighters in the bush united as the *Anya-Nya*[22] guerrilla force (the story of the *Anya-Nya* and other Southern movements is told in chapter 7), and the war entered a new phase.

The military government fell in October 1964. A caretaker government took over under Sirr el Khatim al Khalifa—who had a much gentler style than had been seen in Khartoum for a long time. There was a resurgence of hope and the Southern political movement was re-activated (with Southerners providing three ministers to the caretaker government). A round-table conference was held in Khartoum in March 1965, attended by Southern delegates, delegates from *six* Northern political parties (there had been a confusing proliferation of them) and observers from Uganda, Algeria, Ghana, Kenya, Tanzania and Egypt. The Southerners asked for self-government—or federation as an alternative. The North proposed a system of regional governments. The conference ended indecisively. The caretaker government was replaced by a UMMA–NUP coalition under Mr Mohamed Mahgoub, a former civil engineer, lawyer and Foreign Secretary, whom many regarded as the personification of Northern Arab Sudanese conservatism. He and his government decided to take a tough line in the South and July 1965 was to be remembered as the worst month of the war with mass killings (not to be officially admit-

ted until five years later)[23] at the Southern towns of Juba and
Wau. According to one Southern writer, the resulting cycle of
panic, retaliation and counter-retaliation quickly reduced the
three Southern provinces to a state of anarchy. Refugees fled
across the frontiers into neighbouring countries in such numbers that there were soon reckoned to be at least 100,000
Southern Sudanese in exile.[24]

That was in 1965. In 1966 Premier Mahgoub was replaced
by thirty-year-old Sadiq el Mahdi, the charming and modern-
minded great-grandson of the original Mahdi whose *Ansar*
religious movement still numbers millions in the Sudan. Sadiq
el Mahdi had a reputation for being enlightened. Again there
was hope in the South. Again hope failed. And while the
people of the South suffered in intermittent warfare, the
North suffered the vicissitudes of constant internal political
strife. A bitter quarrel between Sadiq and his traditionalist
uncle, the Imam (head of the *Ansar*), led to Sadiq's replace-
ment by Mahgoub in May 1967. New elections in 1968 saw
Mr Mahgoub again in power—this time heading a coalition
of the Unionist Democratic Party (a merger between the NUP
and the People's Democratic Party), UMMA–Imam (the traditionalist wing of the *Ansar*-dominated UMMA party which
had split over the dispute between the Imam and Sadiq) and
the Southern Front (a Southern party which had been formed
in 1964 and had been in and out of central government).[25]

On 25 May 1969 Mahgoub's government was overthrown
by a revolutionary council under General Nimery; and yet
another chapter of Sudanese history opened. It was at first a
far from happy chapter for the South. The army opened a
series of offensives with—for the first time—Soviet involvement. Soviet Migs, helicopters, bombers and armoury were
used, and Moscow sent military advisers and technicians[26] and
air force pilots and technicians. President Nimery's socialist
government introduced a programme of regional autonomy in
the South, but some frustrations and suspicions remained.
Government spokesmen were later to admit—with apparent
candour and courage—that the suspicions were not altogether

unjustified. After peace negotiations in Addis Ababa in February 1972, there were new hopes, together with formidable challenges.[27]

July 1971 saw an episode which convulsed Khartoum. A communist-led coup overthrew the Nimery regime on 19 July. But seventy-two hours later Nimery had regained control, and he swiftly organised a purge of the Communists and the execution of the ringleaders. Moscow led a world communist campaign of protest against these reprisals. In spite of its vehemence the campaign was not prolonged. But the relations between the Sudan and the Soviet Union began to change.[28]

Notes to this chapter are on page 172

CHAPTER TWO

About the Sudan

Almost everything about the Sudan has been in dispute at one time or another. With an area estimated at between 967,000 and 1,000,000 square miles, the Sudan is the tenth largest country in the world. The Southern Sudan, it is generally recognised, occupies about a quarter of the total area (although some reports put it at nearer one third), making it more than twice the size of, say, Nigeria.

No-one seemed quite sure what the population of the Sudan was at any given time to the nearest hundred thousand or so. The 1956 census (the last one taken in the Sudan to date) showed a total population of 10,262,536—2,783,136 people in the Southern provinces and 7,469,400 in the Northern provinces.[1] A United Nations report published in 1964 gave four population projections for 1971 ranging from a high of 18,150,000 to a low of 14,100,000.[2] The paucity of documentation on births and deaths added to the difficulty of plotting population graphs in the Sudan.[3]

Estimates of the population of the Southern Sudan varied considerably but most reports agreed on a population figure of between four and five million for the South as the war drew to a close.

If the absence of confirmed statistics brought one set of problems for the planners, the fact that there were (according to the 1956 census) nearly 600 tribes in the Sudan gave rise to other problems. In the 1956 census the disparate population of the Sudan was classified into eight major groupings: Arabs 39 per cent; Nilotic (Central Southerners) 20 per cent; Westerners (Western Darfur province) 13 per cent; Nuba 6 per cent; Beja 6 per cent; predominantly Sudanic-speaking tribespeople classified as Western Southerners 5 per cent; Nilo–Hamitic[4] (Eastern Southerners) 5 per cent; Nubians 3 per cent. The remaining 3 per cent, by this reckoning, consisted of Sudanese of foreign origin, foreigners or Sudanese without tribal affiliation (with former West Africans going into the appropriate slot). Various authorities on ethnology, ethnography and demography drew their own conclusions from this. We may happily leave these experts to work out (or argue out) whether the 'Caucasoid' people of the Sudan outnumber the 'Negroid' or the other way round. For practical purposes, Northerners (with the exception of people in Darfur, Kordofan, the Nuba mountains and other 'pockets' who identify themselves as Africans), can be regarded as Arab; and Southerners are predominantly African. This is rough and ready and lacking in scientific precision. But, as one reliable authority points out, it is rare to find anything approaching a pure racial type among any of the peoples of the Sudan. After many racial dispersions, the entire population now varies between the pure Caucasian and the pure Negro type, with the black-skinned people of the South usually being referred to as Negroids. The term 'Arab' has significance in a linguistic and cultural rather than in a racial sense and is used in reference to the result of the recent admixture of indigenous folk and the Arab tribes who settled in the North and Central regions.[5]

There are about 58 principal[6] tribes in the Sudan of which 31 are either Nuba or Westerners and 27 belong to the South. Largest and most powerful are the Dinka (Nilotic), numbering more than a million. Although classified in the 1956 census as Central Southerners, the Dinka—a people rather than a tribe —are divided into several branches and stretch over a wide range of territory (including, for example, the Ngok Dinka in one of the Northern provinces). Next in number are the Nuer, who share with the Dinka the distinction of being the tallest people in the Sudan, averaging well over six feet. Culturally as well as physically, the Nuer are similar to the Dinka.[7] Other

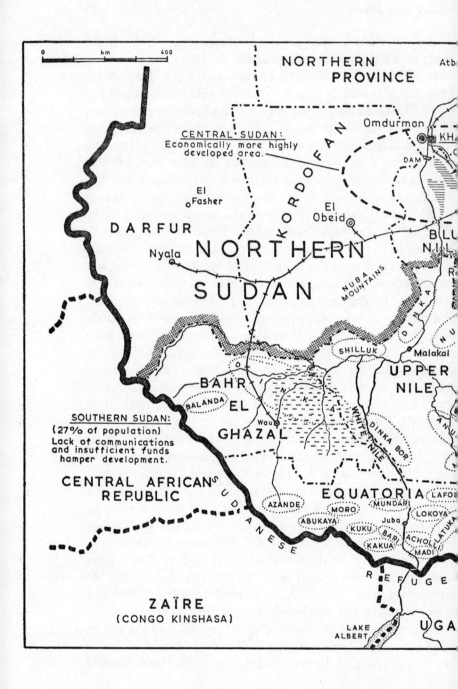

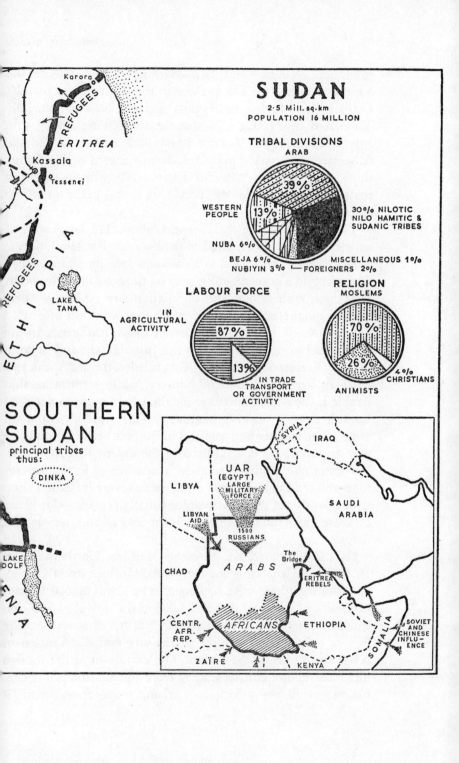

SUDAN

2·5 Mill. sq.km
POPULATION 16 MILLION

TRIBAL DIVISIONS

ARAB

39 %

WESTERN PEOPLE

13%

30% NILOTIC NILO HAMITIC & SUDANIC TRIBES

NUBA 6%

BEJA 6%

NUBIYIN 3%

MISCELLANEOUS 1%

FOREIGNERS 2%

LABOUR FORCE

IN AGRICULTURAL ACTIVITY

87%

13%

IN TRADE TRANSPORT OR GOVERNMENT ACTIVITY

RELIGION

MOSLEMS

70 %

26%

4% CHRISTIANS

ANIMISTS

Karora

REFUGEES

ERITREA

Kassala

Tessenei

ETHIOPIA

REFUGEES

LAKE TANA

SOUTHERN SUDAN

principal tribes thus:

DINKA

LAKE DOLF

KENYA

SYRIA

IRAQ

LIBYA

UAR (EGYPT) LARGE MILITARY FORCE

SAUDI ARABIA

LIBYAN AID

1500 RUSSIANS

ARABS

The Bridge

ERITREA REBELS

CHAD

CENTR. AFR. REP.

AFRICANS

ETHIOPIA

SOVIET AND CHINESE INFLU- ENCE

ZAÏRE

KENYA

SOMALIA

prominent Nilotic (and Nilo–Hamitic) tribes include the
Anuak, the Bari, the Berta, the Bor, the Didinga, the Jur, the
Lotuko, the Murle, the Toposa and the Shilluk (officially
designated pre-Nilotic and traditionally having a king who
rules by divine right). The most prominent among the Sudanic
tribes are the Azande people of South-western Sudan, sometimes described as 'cheerful extroverts',[8] with a tradition
rooted in strong social divisions and strong belief in witchcraft.

The people of the Sudan speak about 114 languages, of
which the South is credited with some 50. For convenience,
Arabic is used in dialects as a common medium of exchange.
According to a government report on the South (published in
1964), more than half the population use Arabic as their
mother tongue while the rest adopt it as a second medium.[9]
There are still, however, residues of English influence in the
South (including such relics as the Juba Hotel); and because
so many literate Southerners, being mission-trained, speak and
write in English, President Nimery, while confirming that
Arabic is the official language for the whole country, declared
English to be a working language of the region.[10] Although
some of the leading personalities in the Southern communities
may appear to be de-tribalised to the extent that they wear
European clothes, have adopted a number of European customs and tend to omit some of the more severe initiation rites,
strong loyalty to tribal principles usually remains—for many
of these principles have significant moral and sociological
bases.

Of the estimated ten to eleven million Northerners (in
1972) an overwhelming majority were Muslims (mostly ortho-
dox Sunni). There were reckoned to be about 50,000 Roman
Catholics—between 3,000 and 4,000 of them Arabs—and considerably more Protestants in the North.[11] But no accurate
figures existed with respect to the size and distribution of
religious groups in the Sudan. The expulsion of the foreign
missionaries and church leaders from the South and the confusion outside the urban areas arising from the war made it

even more difficult to obtain reliable statistics for religious groupings in the three Southern provinces. The great majority of Southerners remained pagan (with many different tribal societies continuing to practise animistic observances which varied from tribe to tribe and sometimes from clan to clan). In 1955 it was estimated that there were 25,000 or more Protestants in the South compared with 180,000 or more Roman Catholics—and around 22,500 Southern Muslims.[12] By the end of 1971, a Roman Catholic spokesman was telling me that there were more than half a million Roman Catholics in the South. The Anglicans, claiming more than 100,000 Anglicans in the South in 1968, said that since then tens of thousands of Southerners had been baptised.

Life in the Sudan continues to be dominated by the Nile, the sun and the rains. The Nile is more than just a river. It is the Sudan's life blood and its main artery. It is a legend and a way of life. While for political and economic reasons and as a result of historical processes (to be discussed elsewhere), it has been found necessary to strive for unification of the Sudan, Nature provided a clearer distinction between North and South than between either part of the Sudan and most of its neighbouring territory. There is the vast barrier of the *Sudd* where masses of floating vegetation continue to block the rivers. There is the great difference in rainfall. It is possible for the traveller, civilian or military, by land or by air, by accident or design, to overstep some of the less clearly defined boundaries between Southern Sudan and Ethiopia or Uganda. But if you are coming from Northern Sudan, the point where the South begins is apparent the moment you reach it. There's the beginning of a great savannah, growing into a large jungle area. The Southern Sudan is fertile and green all the year round, with six months of rainfall—whereas the North is hot and dry (despite a humid atmosphere), with, in most cases, only a few inches of rain from June to September. The grass grows so quickly in the South that it is the subject of local jokes.

The White Nile and the Blue Nile (which, as the British

learn at school, come together at 'Gordon's Khartoum') and
their tributaries continue to provide the major system of communications. Sudan Airways have built up a commendable
service between Khartoum and the principal Southern towns
of Malakal, Wau and Juba; and a railway line now links Wau
(capital of the game-rich province of Bahr el Ghazal) with the
North. But the little steamships still ply their way between
Juda and the North. Taxis now bring the families and their
goods and chattels to the Juba harbour to await the coming of
vessels; but the voyage itself is as slow and hot as it was in days
gone by. In some cases, it is just as difficult to get from one
part of the South to another as from North to South—sometimes more so. The rivers of the Upper Nile and of Bahr el
Ghazal are navigable for only certain months, and which
months these are differs from river to river.

From a military point of view, the South lacks tarmac roads
and much of its terrain is so difficult to negotiate that movement of military, or for that matter civilian, road transport is
difficult and even hazardous. The Southern Wet Plains region
is unsuited for conventional ground operations—except in the
marginal plains between January and March. There are
seasonably favourable terrain conditions for ground operations
in the south-western dissected plains (in the November–April
dry season); but steep-banked streams, scattered hills and
rocky outcrops and dense tropical evergreen forests along
streams near the south-western border are year-round obstacles
to cross-country movement. The south-eastern uplands area is
generally unsuited for ground operations. All in all, the terrain in the Southern Sudan greatly favours guerrilla warfare
and makes counter-insurgency a headache and sometimes a
nightmare.

Khartoum, largest city of the North and capital of the
Sudan, and Juba, largest town of the South and capital of
Equatoria, provide a contrast in urban living. Juba is a very
African town and the presence of mosques along with churches
and of Arab merchants who bring a touch of Arabia into the
market square does not, somehow, make it any less so. Khar

toum, with its mini skyline of tall buildings, its streets seldom free from the sand of the desert, its modern shops and traditional stalls, is very much an Arab city and yet somehow seems to justify the Sudan's claim to be a bridge between the Arab and African worlds. Khartoum means 'snout' and derives its name from the shape of the country where Nile meets Nile. The merciless sun which drives the whole populace into the shade of siesta (although one December morning it was so cold there that I had to wear an overcoat) has created legend after legend for Khartoum.

To illustrate the city's low-key approach to everything— including revolution—a visiting correspondent[13] tells the story popular with the Sudanese in the summer of 1971 of the English journalist in Khartoum for one of the periodic coups. In his dispatch from the city, the Englishman described soldiers driving tanks to the palace for the takeover, dutifully pausing at each traffic light and chatting with bemused pedestrians. Well, the journalist may have invented the story—or more likely the Sudanese invented him. If they had, it wouldn't surprise me. The Sudanese have a gift for smiling at life.

Another report tells of the Sudanese who said laughingly : 'It is no wonder we Sudanese are never nasty to visitors. We don't need to be. We have the weather to do that for us.'[14] For my part, I don't believe the weather has much to do with it. It is just not within the nature of the Sudanese, Northerner or Southerner, Arab or African, even to think of being 'nasty to visitors'. Foreigners are still welcomed in the Sudan with matchless courtesy. It is not only that the language and the mode of greeting have a built-in courtesy. It is not just that no government official in the Sudan would ever dream of sending the visitor away—or indeed of beginning a discussion with him—without first offering him refreshment. It goes far beyond the fact that Sudanese people embarrassed me during my stay in their country by insisting on paying for the taxi, the meal or the drink. To the tradition of both Arab and African hospitality is added a special Sudanese quality. It is

reflected in the story told by a Norwegian newspaper correspondent[15] who had seen a Southern Dinka man at Wau drink
tea at the same table as two Arab civil servants while the war
was raging and had asked him later how he could bear to sit
at the same table as people who killed and robbed his fellow
tribesmen. In the most matter of fact way, the Southerner
replied that, for his people, hospitality was sacred. 'We sit with
the Arabs because this is our country and those who come
from the North are our guests.' I myself have heard similar
comments both from Southerners and (in a different context)
from Northerners. It is reflected in the fact that in the North
or in the South if tragedy strikes a family the neighbours will
gather around as though it was their own suffering. How such
peoples could get involved in the brutality of civil war is a
riddle that runs deep.

If the divisions which had made such a war possible, and
even inevitable, were deep, realists on both sides faced up to
the fact that war had to be ended if the whole country were
not to be crippled. Both sides were paying dearly for it.
According to one estimate in 1971, it cost a million pounds a
month to field the security forces in the South. This could not
be confirmed because the Army High Command is seldom
disposed to take correspondents into its confidence on such
matters. But it was clear that the cost of keeping a substantial
counter-insurgency force in the Southern Sudan must have
been substantial. The war was draining the economy in many
ways. Owing to the dependence on military supplies from the
Soviet Union, much of the Sudan's long-staple premium-
priced cotton (which was usually reckoned to account for anything up to 60 per cent of the country's earnings) was virtually
mortgaged to the Eastern bloc.[16] This dependence on the
Soviet Union—up to the time of the anti-communist purges
of July–August 1971—had been accompanied by a weakening
of economic ties with the West and a serious decline in
reserves. There had been sweeping nationalisation of foreign
and Sudanese-owned companies following the May 1969 coup
largely, it was widely believed, at the instigation of the Com-

munists in the Nimery government and, most probably, of its
Soviet advisers. What was later admitted (privately if not
publicly) to have been over-hasty nationalisation soon began
to hurt. A report by the Bank of Sudan disclosed a deficit of
£ (Sudanese) 5,100,000 in the second quarter of 1970 and a
balance of payments deficit of £ (Sudanese) 9,300,000.[17]

After nationalisation moves had brought industries to a
critical state, General Nimery began slowly and quietly to
revise the policy in favour of at least a partial return to the
private sector. In June 1971 an announcement in Khartoum
said that the Government was planning to remove all obstacles
which were preventing private enterprise from effectively
playing its part in the country's development. And as early as
April of that year the President reopened negotiations with
the World Bank (which he had previously accused of being a
club of imperialists). The change in direction brought divi-
dends. In May 1971 it was reported that Kuwait had given the
Sudan a £20 million (sterling) credit for agricultural machinery and had promised more investments. Saudi Arabia came
along with an offer of aid. It was only the beginning. A British
guarantee of commercial credits up to £10 million was reported and further facilities were on the agenda for discussion.
By the end of September 1971 it was becoming apparent that
the Sudanese were beginning to profit from their anti-Communist drive in terms of Western and pro-Western investment
possibilities.[18]

Some of the planners in Khartoum had long since been
aware of what had to be done to plug the economic drain. A
report was issued by the Ministry of Planning in 1970 tabling
the major targets for the next five years.[19] Since Sudan's
economy is largely based on agriculture and is likely to remain
so in the foreseeable future, the report emphasised the need
for: the introduction of new agricultural crops; the development of new irrigated and rain-fed areas; development of new,
and extension of old, irrigation systems; large-scale agricultural mechanisation; extensive use of chemicals. The Ministry
of Planning appeared to have no illusions about the difficulties

C

of achieving some of its targets and its report made candid
references to the shortcomings of the past years.[20] One of
Khartoum's most prominent importers told me in a private
conversation (in December 1971) that he was optimistic about
certain areas of development. There was an expanding future
in mechanised farming in the North. There were good prospects for increased exports of the primary money-spinner,
cotton, and also for gum arabic, ground-nuts and food oils. In
addition to two existing sugar factories at Knashm el Girba
in Central Sudan and at Guneid, near the Gezira,[21] in the
North, two big new sugar factories were planned—at Saki or
Senner in the North and (provisionally) at Bor in the South—
and world tenders had been invited. The Sudan, he believed,
might well be self-supporting in sugar by 1974 and then turn
to sugar exports. Two big textile mills were already in operation, producing women's and men's wear in about equal
proportions.

The big problem for both North and South was the old
problem of water. Major project in the five-year plan is the
Rahad irrigation scheme to develop the water resources of the
Blue Nile.[22] Estimated costs of the scheme range from £35
million to as much as £50 million. Britain was one of the
countries invited to join a consortium to finance and develop
the scheme—regarded by the Sudanese as their equivalent of
the High Dam project developed by the Russians in Egypt.
Mr Philip Obang (a Southerner), then Sudanese Counsellor
in London, said that the government regarded water as a
priority and was doing its utmost to sink new wells. He said
that there was as much poverty in the North—particularly in
Darfur and Kordofan—as in the South.[23]

The Southern problem was none the less a very special one
—in the economic as well as other spheres. A report by a
neutral body assigned by the government to investigate the
Southern Sudan's economic resources before independence is
still quoted as a guide to the economic potential, needs and
problems of the three Southern provinces. The Southern
Development Investigation Team[24] noted that the area has a

variety of natural resources including agriculture, animal production, forestry and fisheries and hydrological power. According to the report there are opportunities in the South for producing certain commodities required in the North—particularly sugar, tea, coffee, rice, meat and fish. The production of tobacco of acceptable standards was already a possibility. Palm oil was unlikely to be produced for export in the South but planting could be extended to provide the country's requirements for soap-making. No geological survey had yet revealed a mineral deposit of economically workable value, although the possibility that they might one day do so should not be ruled out. Meanwhile, the most suitable industries were those which involved the processing of agricultural products. Oil mills, flour mills, canning and preserving plants were mentioned. In connection with the sugar industry, another possible product was pure alcohol for motor fuel. A hydro-electric scheme on the Nile south of Juba might be used to generate electricity for the production of nitrogenous fertilisers. The papyrus resources of the *Sudd* might be used for the production of fuel briquettes, paper, cellulose, alcohol and acetone. There were possibilities for sisal cordage.

The main obstacles to economic development in the South were the length of communications, shortage of local capital and skilled labour and lack of knowledge and management experience, and the absence of efficient and organised marketing facilities. The improvement of roads and extension of railways were clearly essential. Improvement of road surfaces to all-weather or even all-season standards, especially in the clay soils of the flood region, would be prohibitively costly, but the strengthening of bridges, ramps and culverts to carry heavy diesel transport was considered feasible and necessary, and the improvement of the steamer service was envisaged. Meanwhile, in a wide variety of country (ranging from the permanent papyrus swamps of the *Sudd* to the peaks of the Ematong mountains, from the open grass plains of the Upper Nile province, Eastern Equatoria and the eastern parts of Bahr el Ghazal to the dense forests of the Nile–Congo Divide),

with many untapped resources and many areas uninhabitable,
the people were still largely dependent on subsistence agriculture.[25]

More than a decade and a half later, it all seemed much the
same story. A conference on the social and economic development of the Southern Sudan, held at Juba at the beginning of
1971, showed that the area had considerable latent potential
in sugar, coffee, cotton, tobacco, maize, fishing and cattle—
provided that confidence could be restored.[26]

Under the Nimery regime much has been done. Much more
remains to be done. There were setbacks and disappointments.
There was the sawmill to be set up in Wau for which the
Russians diverted machinery from Syria only to find it would
not work on the local power supply.[27] There was the ambitious
and well-planned £600,000 scheme to resettle semi-nomadic
Dinka tribesmen on a large agricultural estate where their
enormous herds of cattle could be marketed which, reportedly,
attracted only fifty families in a year.[28]

At a seminar at Juba in 1970, the Minister of State for
Southern Affairs[29] admitted, in a moment of candour, that
although two-thirds of the population of the South depended
on animal wealth, the government's Five Year Plan had made
no provision for the development of this wealth. 'Therefore,'
he continued, 'for two-thirds of the Southern population we
have not got much for the next five years.' But (on 20 December 1971) Mr Christopher B. Nyaiiki, Senior Inspector of
Agriculture, Equatoria (a Southerner), told me at Juba that
'economic' agriculture was now being pushed. He was con-
fident, he said, that sugar cane would eventually be the South's
biggest money-spinner. Tea was being grown as a cash crop in
two districts of Equatoria. Four districts in East and West
Equatoria had had such encouraging results with coffee on a
commercial basis that within ten years the South should be
able to export coffee. The tobacco prospects in Equatoria were
such that the Sudan could be self-supporting within five years.
Raw oil would be exported. Self-sufficiency in pineapples was
anticipated, and there were good prospects for chilli pepper.

A report (undated) by A. Wanji, Foreign Affairs Minister and government economic adviser to the (later dissolved) Nile Provisional Government claimed that the Southern Sudan had enough material resources to ensure an economic viability comparable with very few countries in Africa. The report said that in 1958 a Chinese delegation which toured the provinces of Bahr el Ghazal and Upper Nile came to the conclusion, after several experiments, that both areas were capable of producing enough rice cheaply enough for domestic use and for *the whole of the African continent.* The report saw papyrus as an important source of foreign exchange earning and said development of this industry would lead to the establishment of other industries capable of earning foreign exchange. Southern-grown cotton, it claimed, could meet the textile demands of the whole Sudan and save £ (Sudanese) 10 million (annually) in foreign exchange. Coffee, tea, tobacco and sisal could, with adequate development, earn £ (Sudanese) 8 million in foreign exchange for Southern Sudan. According to this report, the Southern Sudan has mineral resources to an extent hitherto undreamed of (and, alleged Mr Wanji, 'kept secret by the Arab government'): rich deposits of uranium in the western district of Bahr el Ghazal; large deposits of copper in the same area; large deposits of iron ore in the Tonj district which could be commercially exploited; large deposits of gold in the eastern part of the Upper Nile province and in many places in Eastern Equatoria; commercially valuable phosphorous in the central region of Equatoria; in Bahr el Ghazal province oil deposits 'suspected around Wau region and... estimated to be important'. This report was written in support of the contention that the Southern Sudan could have a viable economy as a state independent of the North. Its claims, therefore, must be judged in that context.

In any case the problem was how to develop whatever resources existed. In the event, the real economic test for the Southern Sudan would come with the return of hundreds of thousands of refugees and their re-absorption—along with the large population which had taken to the bush—into the mainstream of Sudanese life. It was all too clear that this could be achieved only with an injection of foreign capital and aid on a large new scale.

Notes to this chapter are on page 174

CHAPTER THREE

The 1955 Revolt

Given the tensions, the suspicions, the resentments and the animosities that had built up over the decades, civil war in the Sudan was perhaps inevitable. The disturbances of 1955 precipitated the Sixteen Years' War. The disturbances and the incidents that led to them are outlined in greatest detail and pertinence in the report by the commission of inquiry set up by the government on 8 September 1955.[1] The commission was under the chairmanship of Mr Justice Tawfik Cotran (Indian born). The other two members were a Northerner— Mr Khalifa Mahgoub, General Manager of the Equatoria Projects Board, a former high-ranking police officer—and a Southerner—Chief Lolik Lado, of Liria, Equatoria Province. The report is one of the essential documents of modern Sudanese history.

The incidents which sparked off a mutiny in the Southern Corps of the army involved, among other things, two telegrams, one of which[2] (the commissioners had no hesitation in declaring) was 'false and forged' although some Southerners took it to be authentic. A conference of the (Southern) Liberal Party at Juba in October 1954 had passed a resolution demanding federal status with the North. After the conference the Liberal Party issued a call to all Southern MPs, regardless of party, to form one Southern Bloc to 'pursue the demands of the Southerners' and to meet in Juba in June 1955. Attempts by the government were made to frustrate the conference. The District Commissioner, Yambio (Equatoria) and the Assistant District Commissioner, Yambio, toured their district to obtain from chiefs signatures supporting the government. All forms of pressure were used to obtain their consent, trickery not excluded.[3]

The Assistant District Commissioner summoned thirteen chiefs to his office and sent a telegram in his name on their behalf supporting the government against the Juba conference. The telegram was given much publicity by Radio Omdurman, and so became known to a Zande (Southern) member of Parliament, Elyas Kuze. At a public meeting held at Yambio on 7 July he demanded that the thirteen chiefs who had signed the telegram be dismissed from office. This motion was passed by the meeting. The chiefs demanded Kuze's arrest. He was brought back to Juba, tried with five others by a court of the chiefs he had denounced, and sentenced on 25 July to twenty years' imprisonment on a charge of criminal intimidation. The District Commissioner explained to the court that the maximum sentence they could impose was two years, and the court reluctantly reduced the sentence accordingly. 'We are of the opinion,' commented the commission, 'that the trial was a farce.' Immediately after the sentences were announced, a crowd of about 700 who had assembled in the courtyard staged a demonstration in sympathy with the prisoners. Police and troops were called in to disperse the demonstrators and tear gas was used. The crowd dispersed but small groups raided a shop belonging to a Northerner and beat up a few Northerners, amongst them a pregnant woman who later had a miscarriage.

Yambio is the administrative capital of the Zande district in Equatoria Province. The next day (26 July) disorders occurred at Nzara, a small village sixteen miles west of Yambio and the centre of the Zande cotton industry experiment. Earlier that month the management of the Equatoria Projects Board set up to run the Zande cotton scheme had dismissed *en masse* some 300 Southern workers. The dismissals, accompanied by an increase of Northern technical staff at the scheme, were, in the commission's view, a major blunder.

There was considerable resentment. On the morning of

26 July, sixty of the Southern workmen who had not been dismissed threatened to strike if they were not given more money. A crowd of 250 workmen from the weaving and spinning mills staged a demonstration. They were joined by hooligans, unemployed and other civilians, armed with spears, bows and arrows. The crowd swelled to a thousand. Police and army reinforcements were rushed to the scene, where the crowd were looting shops. Soldiers opened fire with rifles, a sten gun and a bren gun. Two Northern merchants shot at the mob with an elephant gun and a .22 rifle. Eight people in the crowd died and a number were wounded. 'If there was some confidence left in the administration,' the commissioners commented, 'it then disappeared completely.' [4]

The report found that the situation at Nzara was mishandled. Instead of an immediate inquiry being made, a threatening ultimatum from Khartoum was circulated and broadcast. On 7 August, a conspiracy to mutiny in the Southern Corps was discovered. The authorities were too weak to make any arrests in the army immediately, but two civilians, who appeared to have had a finger in the mutiny were arrested in Juba. A demonstration took place with the mob demanding the release of the accused. The District Commissioner was assaulted by the mob and it had to be dispersed with tear gas. By now the administration had lost the confidence of every shade of opinion in the South and frantic calls were made to Khartoum to send in Northern troops.

Khartoum, neither understanding nor appreciating the situation, was reluctant, but finally flew in a company which arrived ahead of its equipment and support. Rumours multiplied and the last straw came when, for reasons of prestige, the army command in Equatoria decided to persist in their order that No 2 Company Southern Corps should move to Khartoum when they and everybody else in Equatoria knew that the Company would refuse to obey the orders and would mutiny—and when the only reliable force left to preserve law and order and to protect life and property was a company of 200 Camel Corps Nubas,[5] crippled by the lack of equipment, transport and mortar support, in a province as large in area as Italy.[6]

The men of the Southern Corps were all Southerners. There were at the time nine Southern officers in the Corps and twenty-four Northern officers, the majority of whom were of higher rank. The first group of Northern troops arrived by air on 10 August. Many Southern civilians took their families and left Juba as they thought Northern troops were coming to kill them. Eighteen days later mutiny broke out at Torit, Equatoria. The mutineers broke into arms and ammunition stores and then started hunting for Northern officers and men trapped in the town. There was shooting and looting—which got worse the next day. Many Southern civilians left Torit in panic—and an estimated fifty-five of them, including many children, were drowned trying to cross the river Kinyetti outside Torit. Some Southern Corps soldiers who had escaped from Juba (and one at least of whom had been implicated in the alleged conspiracy) spread the news that the Arab *Haggana*[7] had fired at them and had killed a number of Southern soldiers and civilians. Exaggerated reports of heavy casualties in Juba had the effect of exciting the Southerners to take revenge.

Meanwhile the police had persuaded Northern merchants and their families to come for protection to the prison cells, where they locked them in. On the morning of 20 August a lorry-load of Southern mutineers invaded the prison and fired shots into the cells. Of the thirty-six Northern merchants in the men's cell, nine were killed and five injured. In the women's cell, five merchants who were with their wives were shot dead. Four Northern women and eight children, including a newly-born baby, were also killed. Eleven Northerners were taken to hospital where Catholic missionaries took care of them. Two Northern officers joined them. A Southern officer ordered the Northern officers to be taken back to the army cells and they were killed outside the cells. Two Northern merchants who were let out of their cell to bury the dead officers were also shot dead. A local Catholic missionary heard of this outrage and came and took the remaining survivors to the mission.

All over Equatoria Northerners were killed in the August disturbances. The commission's report put the total number of Northern fatalities at 261—259 of them in Equatoria, including 78 at Torit. The report gave names and occupations, and added that, since it had not been possible to compile a complete record of non-fatal casualties, they had decided to omit these figures altogether from their report. All towns and villages in Equatoria outside Juba were affected, and chaos prevailed for over fourteen days. Only Northern Sudanese persons and property were attacked, and Southern soldiers, policemen, warders and civilians took part in the murders, arson and looting. Known Southern fatalities for the same period, excluding the 55 drowned at Torit, numbered 20—11 in Equatoria and 9 at Malakal (Upper Nile Province).

It is clear that most of the killings were a direct result of rumours that Southern civilians in Juba had been massacred. The commissioners listed no more than four Southern deaths at Juba. In some areas where Northern men were killed, their women and children were unharmed. Some Southerners saved Northerners from death by calming the rioters. The report gave instances of gallant attempts by individual Southerners to save Northern lives. Details were also given of many shocking incidents. At Kateri, a small village about forty miles from Torit, the chief tricked a loyal police corporal into releasing a Northern survivor, then had the Northerner speared to death. At another village, Kapoeta, 110 miles east of Torit, a Northern officer who had been promised that he would be treated as a prisoner of war was murdered in his bath tub. At Tali, north of Juba, a Northern merchant's 11-month-old baby was said to have been taken from his mother and fatally injured by a medical assistant who swung him by the leg and banged him on the ground.[8] At Yei the District Commissioner was among those shot and the body of an officer who was shot with him was set on fire. None of the thirty-two Northerners killed at Yei was buried until the Belgian Red Cross Society from

Aba sent some medical attendants to disinfect and bury the
bodies.[9] At Loka, a small village about sixty-five miles from
Juba, when two houses were set on fire, the Northerners in
the house, many of them women and children, ran into the
forest. According to the report, they were followed into the
forest where some were shot and two women were speared to
death.[10] At Meridi the District Commissioner was stripped of
his jacket and shot dead along with five other Northerners.
But Northern teachers and their families at Meridi had their
lives spared thanks to the intervention of Southern students
and two British teachers.[11]

At Nzara—scene of the 26 July disorders—all Northerners
who had not escaped were rounded up and sent to Yambio
prison. There were thirty men and several women and children. On the morning of 20 August the thirty Northerners had
a rope tied around their necks and were marched into an open
space. Sixteen policemen and warders opened fire on them.
Seventeen were killed immediately, and the wounded were
shot as they were dying. Four Northerners somehow succeeded
in disentangling themselves from the rope and escaped into
the bush. They were chased and one of them was killed. Many
other Northerners, who were unable to escape from Yambio,
were chased and murdered by troops, warders and police.[12]

The report found, however, that in the Upper Nile the
authorities had generally handled the situation with ability
and foresight. Except at Malakal, the police had generally
remained loyal.

In Bahr el Ghazal Province when tension mounted at Wau,
the Governor, the Deputy Governor and other high-ranking
Northern officials, decided that the situation was absolutely
hopeless and left the town by steamer. The report paid tribute
to Southern members of Parliament and the Chief Inspector
of Police (Gordon Muortat) who among other Southerners did
their best to maintain law and order and succeeded in
preventing casualties.

On 20 August a state of emergency was proclaimed in the
three Southern provinces. On 22 August the Prime Minister,

Mr Ismail El Azhari, called on troops at Torit to surrender. They refused and requested that Northern troops be evacuated from the South. The Prime Minister refused to do this. Then Sir Knox Helm, the (British) Governor-General, who was on leave in Scotland when the mutiny broke out, returned to Khartoum and sent a message to the mutineers repeating the Prime Minister's assurance that there would be a full investigation into the causes of the mutiny and they would be properly treated as military prisoners. The mutineers requested the Governor-General to evacuate the Northern troops from Juba or send British troops to the South. On 26 August Sir Knox Helm sent the mutineers a final warning to surrender; and on 27 August they agreed to do so.

On 31 August when Northern troops entered Torit they found it virtually empty. Southern soldiers had evacuated the town completely as the surrender negotiations were going on. 'They were convinced that Northern troops were going to kill them,' said the report. So began a resistance movement in the Southern bush. The rest is history.

The report of the commission of inquiry found that the direct causes of the 1955 disturbances were:

1. The forged telegram ordering persecution of Southerners, alleged to have been written by the Prime Minister, Sayed Ismail El Azhari, around the beginning of July 1955.
2. The interference of some administrators in Equatoria in political affairs.
3. Loss of confidence due to the farcical trial of the Southern MP Elyas Kuze.
4. The shooting of Southerners at Nzara on 26 July 1955, which many Southerners regarded as the beginning of a war.
5. Inaction when the conspiracy to mutiny was discovered and Khartoum's misjudgement of the situation in Torit.
6. The Southerners' extreme disappointment and frustration when, among other things, 'Sudanisation' gave them only 6 out of a total 800 senior government posts vacated by

the departing British in 1954, and their consequent fear of
political domination.[13]

7. The circulation of false or exaggerated rumours and the
corresponding lack of effective government propaganda to
allay fears and misapprehensions.

The most significant feature of the report was the outlining
of basic causes of hostility between Northerners and Southerners which led to disturbances and exacerbated them. Some
of them remained relevant to the quest for peace seventeen
years later. Among other things, the commissioners blamed
British administrative policy until 1947 for preventing the
Sudanese from knowing each other, working with each other
and learning from each other. The report also condemned the
missionaries who, with most of the South's education in their
hands and for their own purposes, had thrown in their influence in favour of the above policy.

It pointed out that, for political, financial, geographical and
economic reasons the Northern Sudan had progressed quickly
in every field (local government, irrigation schemes, health,
higher education, industrial development) while the Southern
Sudan lagged far behind. This marked difference in development between two such different peoples of one country had
inevitably created a feeling in the under-developed people,
justifiably or not, that they were being cheated, exploited and
dominated.[14]

For all these reasons, the commissioners found it hardly
surprising that the Southern Sudanese had no feeling of common citizenship with the Northern Sudanese and that their
loyalties remained, as they had always done, to their own tribe
alone. It was only in the past year or so that the average
Sudanese had been at all politically conscious and, as was only
to be expected from political beginners, this consciousness was
regional rather than national.[15]

All the evidence suggested that the real trouble in the South
was political and not religious. Neither the historical fact of
the slave trade (used by different people for different pur-

poses) nor the differences in religion had played any part in the disturbances. Christians, Pagans and Moslems had taken part in the Equatoria disturbances; in fact some of the leaders of the anti-Northern propagandists had been Southern Moslems.[16]

The report also drew attention to a matter which it said was not one of the direct causes of the disturbances but had created ill-feeling among the Southerners and caused loss of confidence in the administration. This was the conduct of some Northern traders, or *Gallaba*, in the Southern Sudan. Although Southern accusations against the traders were frequently prompted by envy rather than any just grievance, it was unfortunately true that many Northern Sudanese regarded the Southerners as inferior and the *Gallaba* were no exception. The traders often called Southerners *abeed* (slaves). This practice, which was widespread in the three Southern provinces, had created great ill-feeling among Southerners.[17]

The report did not comment on the controversial issue of the British role in the upheaval of 1955. The allegation has been made not infrequently by, and on behalf of, Southerners that the promise made by Sir Knox Helm's deputy that 'legitimate grievances of the Southerners would be heard if they would lay down their arms' was never kept. Eight thousand Northern troops were airlifted to the South in RAF planes, and Sir Knox Helm left the country on 15 December never to return. Those of the mutineers who did not escape into the bush were tried and shot, and even the promise of personal safe-conduct made to Lieutenant Reynaldo Loyela (the leader of the revolt) did not save him from being executed early in 1956.[18]

The report of the commission of inquiry was widely commended both by Northerners and Southerners for its objective and, on the whole, accurate assessment. Where the significance of the report lay depended, to some extent, on where one stood. It could be, and was, quoted as evidence of irresponsible and rash behaviour by Southern politicians which set a bad example to other Southerners;[19] a series of blunders by North-

ern administrators; and of many other imprudences. Many
Southerners felt that the excesses on the Southern side were
overshadowed by the ferocity of the reprisals that followed
over a far longer period (the inquiry was into the causes,
rather than the effects, of the 1955 disturbances). Some Southerners have also felt it necessary to point out that the commission was set up by one Prime Minister and its findings
(which disclosed serious shortcomings on the part of his
administration) were made public by a new Prime Minister
of an opposing political party. This does not, however, detract
from the fact that a Sudanese government did set up an
impartial commission of inquiry and a Sudanese government
did bring out into the open candid comments on matters
which it would have been wrong and cynical to conceal. That
many of the shortcomings and evils exposed—like raw nerves
—by the report, continued to exist long after its publication
is purely the responsibility of the actors in the drama—not of
its chroniclers.

Notes to this chapter are on page 175

CHAPTER FOUR

Violence and Suffering

It was a bitter war. There were no verifiable statistics on the killings. There were only estimates. Deaths from disease, including 'starvation' (a term medical authorities hesitate to use as a direct cause of death) were believed to be no less, and perhaps more, numerous. A report in 1967 put the estimated number of black Southerners killed between 1963 and 1966 at more than half a million.[1] In a letter to the Pope dated 25 May 1970, General Joseph Lagu, leader of the *Anya-Nya* guerrillas, wrote: 'Already more than 500,000 men, women and children have perished—either shot dead, burnt alive in their huts or died from famine and disease.'[2] By early 1971, United Nations sources were said to be estimating a total of over 500,000 dead.[3] Southern Sudanese at that time, on the other hand, were claiming that a further million had died in massacres or from indirect, war-related causes such as starvation and untreated wounds.[4] Many other reports gave the 500,000 figure for killings, but some observers thought the estimate exaggerated. Government spokesmen in Khartoum at the end of 1971 certainly thought the half-a-million estimate an exaggeration.[5]

The vast majority of the victims were Southern civilians. Details of their suffering came from Southern sources and sources sympathetic to the South. Some Northerners who sought an end to the strife were sincere enough to admit that ugly deeds had been done. But they accused the *Anya-Nya* of having murdered Southerners who refused to co-operate with, or pay taxes to, the rebels. Some Southerners agreed that there had been cases where Southern civilians had been killed or

D

injured by guerrillas. One Southerner who seemed to be as objective as it is humanly possible to be in a situation which so stirs the emotions told me he had personally seen this happen. But all these Southerners emphasised that such incidents were on a small scale compared with the killings and maimings by the Army. Wanton killing of civilians was against the declared policy of the Nimery administration. One must therefore assume that during the Nimery regime such killings were carried out, in the main, without official sanction. Undoubtedly in many cases individual army units acted under a sense of provocation. There were grim reprisals for *Anya-Nya* raids on army posts, and ferocious counter-reprisals. It was the ugly, naked face of war.

The most notorious incident was the alleged massacre at a village called Banja (sometimes spelled as Banza or Bansa) on the Sudan–Congo frontier, on 26 July 1970. According to accounts given by survivors to a Norwegian television reporter, Per Oyvind Heradstveit, a unit of Sudanese soldiers burst in on a Christian community of the indigenous Bakerole Church while they were at prayer. The patrol consisted of twenty-one men, all with automatic weapons. They tied the curate with his hands behind his back to a fragile chair. Another group went from hut to hut using knives. Those inhabitants who were still alive, most of them women and children, were brought into the chapel where they were tied to chairs with a thick rope. An officer gave the command. As he left the church, he is alleged to have said to the captives: 'We're shooting you in your house of worship. Let your God come and save you.' Then the patrol took up positions on the other side of the church. They emptied one or two magazines apiece. Stifled cries of pain were heard. Not all were dead. 'Light it,' came the order. A few seconds later the church with its straw roof was in flames. Fifty died in the church. Some of the inhabitants had hidden outside the church. They tried to flee. The soldiers fired round after round at them till they disappeared in the grass. Some bled to death and were never found. But fourteen managed to get to the hospital in Abᴉ

(inside the Congo). 'They told us about Banja,' says Heradstveit.[6] He and television photographer Oystein Stabrun, after
interviewing and photographing survivors at the hospital,
were taken to the scene. 'We could see the bones of a child's
hand, part of a skull,' writes Heradstveit. 'The charred remains of a bible lay in the sand.' The television team took
photographs and brought back with them to Oslo empty
cartridges, the bible and a piece of the charred rope with
which the victims were allegedly tied.

In the following months, similar accounts appeared in the
world press.[7] The only difference in the reports was that some
put the number of dead at twenty-seven, with fourteen seriously wounded, and some gave the date of Banja as 23 July
instead of 26 July. These were the first corroborated reports
of mass killing in the Southern Sudan since Nimery's National
Revolutionary Council took power in May 1969.[8] A delegation
from the Southern Sudan Liberation Front presented the
President of the United Nations General Assembly with a
petition on 17 December 1970, which simply noted that 'on
23 July 1970, 27 people were killed at prayer'.[9]

Four months previously, on 18 September 1970, the late
Joseph Garang, the Southerner and Communist executed in
1972 for his part in the Communist coup, issued a statement[10]
describing the Banja reports as false and unbelievable. 'Everybody knows that there are no churches in villages either in the
North or the South.' Southern nationalists[11] commented that
the Minister of Southern Affairs' statement demonstrated how
out of touch he was with his own people. A former missionary
told me that Mr Garang's denial was based on a technicality.
In churches throughout the Southern Sudan the same building was used as a school and as a church and there were
hundreds of such buildings which became churches when
people prayed in them. I was told elsewhere that one prominent Southerner associated with the government was shocked
into tears when shown the burnt rope, prayer book and spent
cartridges. When I asked Major-General Mohamed Abdul
Gadir, then Chief of Staff of the Sudan army, about the Banja

incident, he said he had no knowledge of it. I told him I had
seen what purported to be photographic evidence and also the
burnt rope and the charred (and apparently bayoneted) bible.
The General was then frank enough to reply: 'It is possible
that it did happen and possible that it didn't.' He added: 'If
it did, soldiers must have gone into the building in search of
Anya-Nya and not known there were civilians inside.' [12]

Mr Ateny Mudrateny Pajokdit, a veteran Southern politician and guerrilla fighter, was reported to have said[13] that
since 1969 soldiers had massacred entire villages or segments
of their populations in at least 212 cases. In Bahr el Ghazal
province all 700 (estimated) inhabitants of a Dinka village,
Marial Aguog, were machine-gunned; an estimated 2,000
people were reportedly killed in villages surrounding the
police post at Ulang, nine miles north of Nasir, in Upper Nile
province, and their cattle were driven north; in November
1970, at Morta in Equatoria province, about 800 young men
of the village were allegedly killed and their women maimed.
According to the *Anya-Nya* commander-in-chief, General
Lagu, an ex-member of one of Sudan's Parliaments, reached
one of their camps in December 1970 and reported that in the
province of Bahr el Ghazal between April and August 1970
500 civilians were killed in Abiei and Bentiu districts; 600 in
Gogrial; 700 in Aweil; 500 in Tonj; 500 in Rumbek; 400 in
Yiroli; 300 in Western District, and 200 in Raga. He went on
to report that 100,000 head of cattle had been killed or confiscated by the enemy during the same period in Bahr el
Ghazal.[14] According to a Norwegian correspondent[15] a Southerner who had been a Member of Parliament in Khartoum
for a total of ten years alleged that about 6,000 houses had
been burned down, 200 persons killed and 50 women raped
in Aweil from August 1970 to January 1971. Those responsible were said to be irregular forces operating in the name of
the government. Another report[16] described how six members
of one of the leading Dinka families, including the Paramount
Chief of Ngok Dinka, Abdalla Deng, were killed by soldiers
in cold blood on 17 September 1970.

A Southern Sudanese refugee on the Ethiopian border and an *Anya-Nya* supporter in London gave me corresponding accounts of the Akobo affair in July 1971. Akobo is a town in the Upper Nile province of Southern Sudan close to the Ethiopian border. The elementary school principal, Martin Mirich, was killed outside the town. Both versions said he had been forced into a car, taken away and shot. Angered by this, the *Anya-Nya* launched an attack in the area. As a reprisal for the *Anya-Nya* attack thirty-nine Southerners were taken out of prison at Akobo and machine-gunned. The refugee on the Ethiopian border said he had personally seen thirteen 'Arab' soldiers under a captain, whom he named, marching through the town, turning their machine-guns on all people who wore good clothes.[17] Some of these and similar reports were corroborated by other sources. In other cases confirmatory evidence did not appear to be available and some may have been exaggerated.

After 1970, according to Southern allegations, the army, for political reasons, began to change its tactics from open killings to kidnappings, 'pulling people out of their homes, throwing their bodies into rivers or by the riverside and blaming the killings on the rebels'.[18] Southern sources alleged, in August 1970,[19] that a number of refugees who had returned from abroad and had been resettled in so-called peace camps at Nasir were put into military vehicles and told they were being taken to Malakal (provincial capital of the Upper Nile province) to be employed or on transfer. A day later the bodies of six of these men, with bullet wounds, were found floating in the River Sobat. The names of the five who were recognised were recorded in the Southerners' report. Major-General Gadir told me he had no knowledge of such incidents. 'We have had hundreds of complaints and each one is investigated. Brutality against civilians is forbidden and any soldier committing such acts would be charged with a criminal offence.'[20] Since the purge of August 1971 and a new phase of the government programme in the South under the ministry of the reasonable and moderate Southerner, Abel Alier, there were far fewer allegations concerning the treatment of civilians.

The report of the commission of inquiry into the disturbances in the Southern Sudan in August 1955 showed that there were both immediate and deep-seated causes for the 1955 revolt. Reports of atrocities committed against Northerners in Equatoria province were as insistent and as shocking as any of the reports of atrocities against Southerners—and they included allegations that Northern men, women and children were butchered or whipped and skinned and hung from trees.[21] The memory of these killings fanned the fury of reprisals (said to include daily firing squads) for months and even years to come.

A survivor of the 1955 revolt, Benjamine Odominyanf Loful, is quoted in the book, *The Nile Turns Red*,[22] as describing how for a complete month he and other Southerners were carried from the prison every night to a foothill, three miles outside Juba Township, and brutally beaten. They were allegedly trodden on by Arab officers as they lay bound hand and foot in heavy iron chains. Several prisoners were said to have died in their cells. In order to terrorise prisoners and obtain confessions, officers were said to have stubbed cigarettes out in their eyes and tortured them by abusing their sexual organs. Before being taken into the prison ward for their turn of the ordeal, new detainees were kept in heavy chains inside locked cells for several days or even weeks, without food, water or being taken to the toilet. The book also alleges that in Yambio district Police Officer Placido Oboke had his eyes put out and after a week his hands and feet were cut off and he was left bleeding in a cell for a month before being executed.

A similar fate befell Marcelo Andal, a prison officer in the same district, who had been accused by a Northern woman of not having saved the life of her husband. An officer is alleged to have dug out the eyes of four Southern boys with a penknife before their execution. At Malakal, Upper Nile province, at the end of 1956, another survivor of the 1955 revolt, James Kockweth, told the author of *The Nile Turns Red* how he and nine other men were tied against poles in front of machine guns and left there for two weeks. 'Each day the soldiers gave us ten strokes each, while others spat on our bleeding wounds after having put salt on them. It was not enough to suffer their whipping. We had to kiss the whips and say "Thank you".' A Southern priest, Father Gabriel Dwatuka, described how, on 18 October 1955, at Yambio, his cassock was torn off him and he was lashed with his own rosary beads and then with a whip while he hung from a rope.

In a statement given to the Sudan African Liberation Front (SALF), Francis Lotwari, formerly Chief of the village of Tirrangore in Equatoria province, described how soldiers and policemen searching for the 'Rain Maker', Lomiluk Lohide, arrested his brother, Sohoti Lohide. He was brought to Torit and interrogated on the whereabouts of the Rain Maker (who, unknown to him, had crossed into Uganda). Sohoti was beaten unconscious. When he seemed on the point of death, soldiers tied him in a sack and threw him in an incinerator. Towards dawn Sohoti regained consciousness and managed to crawl to the Catholic Mission, a distance of one and a half miles, on his knees. He was treated secretly at the mission dispensary.[23]

It is generally agreed, both in the North and in the South, that the worst period of *calculated* repression was during the Abboud military regime (November 1958 to October 1964). For the South, the military regime meant the silencing of any talk of federation. Every enlightened Southerner was classified as a politician and therefore a potential trouble-maker. At that time, according to one Southern writer, 'enlightened' appears to have meant anything from being educated to merely being neatly dressed and failing to behave as an inferior to Northerners.[24]

Years later members of the Nimery Administration condemned the excesses of the Abboud regime. But for details of these excesses we have to rely on reports from Southern sources and missionaries, whose concern was often personal and emotional (and at a time when foreign observers were almost entirely unaware of the conflict in the Southern Sudan).

The reports brought a dismal picture of burnings of homes, killings and torturings in what was described as collective punishment. Teachers and schoolboys appeared to have been singled out for punishment.[25] In a memorandum written on 26 November 1962, William Deng (Nhial), Executive Member of the Sudan African Closed Districts National Union (SACDNU), told of a general strike then in progress throughout the South by schoolboys and secondary students in protest against discrimination and cruel treatment by Arab teachers. According to Mr Deng, the schoolboys were rounded up by soldiers and some of them had their teeth pulled out by pliers. Other reports told of the killing of teachers, including headmasters, and schoolboys, although many escaped across the border.

All this—together with the closing down of all schools in the South on General Abboud's orders, in 1964, and the alleged plot on Christmas Eve, 1960, to carry out mass arrests of Southern politicians—was quoted as lending weight to the views of Richard Owen, formerly British Governor of Bahr el Ghazal, who once said that while, for him, 'genocide' was an abused exaggerated word, it was a charge which could be made against the Khartoum government in so far as they—or the Northern soldiers with government connivance—had tried to liquidate educated Southerners and potential leaders as a matter of policy.

When in spite of the Abboud regime's attempts to end rebellion in the South the rebels organised themselves as the *Anya-Nya* movement in 1963, army action against civilians was stepped up with the object of intimidating people suspected of co-operating with, or even knowing about, the rebels. Some of the allegations are horrifying. The Grinti prison in Bahr el Ghazal gained an infamous reputation. Reports by Verona Fathers told of floggings at this prison and tortures—including the use of metal rings and metal balls which almost pushed the eyes out of the head—to get confessions. One of the tortures involved the use of a red chilli, pepper or paprika powder known as *shatta* or *citeta*. A bag was filled with this and the victim's head was forced into the bag and kept there until he could not breathe any longer and his eyes were inflamed. During such ordeals beatings continued. *Shatta* was also rubbed into raw wounds and body openings. Reports of *shatta* torture also came from the then President of the Sudan African National Union, Joseph Oduho, a Southerner who had narrowly escaped execution after the 1955 revolt. In a memorandum presented by the Union to the Commission of the Organisation of African Unity for Refugees at Kampala on November 1964, Mr Oduho alleged that nearly all Southern police warders, policemen, officers and other officials were arrested in Wau on 12 January 1964. A hundred and five were tried. At Grinti, before the trials, the arrested men, stripped naked, were forced to put their heads into chilli powder. Some were beaten until bleeding and their bodies smeared with soaked chillies. Mr Siro Maa, an accountant, and Mr John Majok Nang, a prison warder, were among those flogged to death on 15 and 19 January. Mr Oduho's report gave names of Northern captains, a colonel and police chief inspector alleged to have taken part personally in the torture. Other people were allegedly tortured by having flesh sliced off their bodies, while some had their flesh roasted with hot irons. Others were said to have been suspended from a string head down and beaten unconscious and even to death.[26]

Then there was the case of Albino Bambala, a schoolteacher, of Deim Zubeir, in the province of Bahr el Ghazal, whose eyeballs, according to the relatives who buried him in February 1964, were entirely obscured by red pepper.[27] At the same time, the skin had been flayed from his back. Another schoolteacher at Deim Zubeir was allegedly tortured in the schoolhouse in early March 1964 by soldiers who first cut off one of his arms, then one of his legs and finally slit his throat. His wife was ordered to bury his body and get out of her government-supplied house. She was allegedly sexually assaulted by the soldiers and beaten. *Shatta* was then rubbed into the open wounds on her body and on her children.

In the Central Council on 11 March 1964, Gobrial Kaw

Atir and Alfred Wol made charges of torture with red pepper after the rebel attack on Wau. These accusations, which are repeated in detail and circumstance in the *Answer*[28] to the *Black Book* (written by Catholic missionaries expelled from the Sudan, and published in Verona in September 1964) were categorically denied by the Minister responsible, Sayed Ziyada Arbab.

Some of the reported killings during the period appeared to have had no motivation at all. There was twelve-year-old Cirillo Angol, of Lorewo village, who was sent into a maize field by his father to scare birds away, was seized by soldiers (who had heard that rebels had taken maize from the field), and shot in the presence of his parents and other children. There was a man of seventy allegedly shot in cold blood in his hut forty-two miles from Yei in Equatoria. There were four young men of Ngangala who were carrying a sick person to hospital at Lirya (Equatoria) and who were arrested, beaten and ended in hospital themselves. A teacher alleged that two Southerners on bicycles were stopped by Arab police, who took away their bicycles; and when they asked for the return of their bicycles were shot on the spot and used by the police for bayonet practice.

In August 1959, according to Mr Oduho, at Katire village a Northern police sergeant saw some children playing with rocks and asked them if they were monkeys. When told that they were a group of children, he shot one—a six-year-old boy. The case was heard at Torit by a District Commissioner, who told the father of the boy that the case was simple because the sergeant did not know if what he was shooting at was a human being or a monkey. The Commissioner then pulled off two chevrons from the sergeant and said to the child's father: 'Are you happy now that I have demoted the man?' The sergeant was transferred to Khartoum. The District Commissioner offered the father £20 compensation which he refused. Unbelievable? But Mr Oduho attested in his memorandum that he was present in court and he named the District Commissioner.

The Abboud military regime suceeded in antagonising not only the South but the North. In Khartoum in October 1964, violent riots arose over protests against the government's harshness in the South. A Khartoum university student was among three people killed. The Abboud regime fell. The caretaker government of Sirr el Khatim flung open the political prisons and the torture camps. On 10 November 1964, he called for a cease-fire. Two days later Clement Mboro, Minister of the Interior in the new government and a highly regarded Southern Front leader, persuaded the *Anya-Nya* to accept the cease-fire.

Unhappily the truce did not last for long. The new Prime Minister made a fact-finding tour of the South to pave the way to better relations. But he was soon to be informed (in a letter from the Southern Front) that a few days after his visit government troops killed sixteen people in the Thiet Council area in the Jur River district, including the court president and two schoolmasters. All sixteen alleged victims were named.[29] Other killings were alleged to have taken place on Christmas Eve and on New Year's Eve. Mr Louis Adwok Bong, member of the Supreme Council of State, was at the Round Table Conference which opened on 30 March 1965, to try to find an amicable solution to the problem of the Southern Sudan. Mr Bong, who represented the Upper Nile province, was informed that a systematic destruction of the province had begun on the very day the conference opened. He left on 10 April to check, and on 22 April reported to Sirr el Khatim and the Council of Ministers that he had found that his own village of Agodo (on the west bank of the Nile in Kodok district) had been utterly and systematically destroyed by the armed forces stationed at Kodok. A number of other villages were wholly or partly destroyed. Mr Bong's four-year-old niece had been killed. Twelve persons died in one village, nine in another (names given). 'Even worse conditions exist in other parts of the South,' said Mr Bong's note. He then went on to demand the immediate lifting of the state of emergency in the South.[30]

In spite of this, the Sirr el Khatim government was to be remembered by many as a benevolent one. But the Round Table talks fizzled out and the caretaker government fell all too quickly. In June 1965 a new government was formed under Mr Mohamed Mahgoub, who took the line that guerrillas had to be subdued rather than parleyed with. (In a speech at Khartoum on 10 June 1965, Mr Mahgoub was quoted as undertaking to stamp out 'the terrorist gangs which abused security'.) July 1965 was the worst month of the whole war for killings in the South. On 4 July, 150 Southerners were allegedly killed at Torit. On 8 July there was a night of shooting and burning at Juba. According to one report from the Southern Front, the Officer Commanding Troops at Juba told the President and Vice-President of the Southern Front Central Committee a week later that fifty-six persons had been killed. Estimates of the number of dead ranged from 1,019 to 3,000 killed.[31] That killings on a mass scale took place in Juba seems beyond doubt. There were conflicting reports on what exactly happened, how it happened, and why it happened. The version collected by the Southern Front delegates from official sources was that a soldier had been attacked by a group of Southern civilians believed to be rebels and that shots were fired against the Officer Commanding Troops' house; the army then carried out an operation in which 'it was extremely difficulty to differentiate between the ordinary citizens and outlaws'. The unofficial version given in most reports on the Juba massacre was that a quarrel broke out between a Northern sergeant and a Southern hospital dresser over a transistor radio. The sergeant was injured and this led to massive reprisals. But some Southern sources made allegations[32] that the army had received instructions to kill all educated persons in Juba. Northern soldiers in Juba were said to have gone to the cinema on the night of the killings. Reports differed on whether they carried their guns with them or picked them up after they had heard about the sergeant's injuries. It was agreed that shooting went on through the night and that soldiers set fire to many houses.

After Juba came Wau. Southern eye-witnesses described how seventy-six people had been killed by soldiers while they were attending a reception after a double wedding on 11 July. A report by Mr Aggrey Jaden, then President of the Sudan African Liberation Front, gave the names and designations of fifty-five of the victims.[33] Wau was followed by Rumbek on 20 July 1965, when soldiers allegedly shot up the town. The death toll was alleged to have run into the hundreds. At Warajwok (six miles from Malakal), on 5 August 1965, the men of the village were allegedly rounded up and 187 shot dead by soldiers. A Southern Front report gave fifty of the names. The women and children of the village were un-harmed and taken to a peace zone.

Five years later Mr Abel Alier (in an address at Kampala) said that he saw these excesses as stemming from the events in 1955 when innocent and often well-meaning Northerners had been murdered in the South. Some of the Northern officials still in positions of authority in the South had seen friends, even close relatives, killed before their eyes. It was then per-haps hardly surprising that when the Southerners were in much the same predicament in 1965 as the Northerners had been ten years earlier, many of the security officials from the North should choose to turn a blind eye. Such a view could be interpreted as a remarkably tolerant and perceptive comment by a Southerner about a situation charged with emotion—the kind of leap across the gulf of bitterness which the leadership of both sides had to make if the hatreds of the past were to be removed from Sudanese thinking.

Once again there was hope of relief from the violence that had plagued the South when an apparent progressive, Sadiq el Mahdi, took over the government in June 1966. Once again the lull was not to last. In October 1966 (according to an American journalist who spent at least three years in the Sudan teaching and writing[34]) troops machine-gunned 340 dancers at a place called Tali. William Nhial, a member of SANU (Sudan African National Union), who went to the South to prepare for elections and reportedly had safe-conduct papers from the Prime Minister's office, was killed—allegedly by government troops.

In the Torit district of Eastern Equatoria, according to pro-Southern sources,[35] 400 people were killed between 27 and 29 December 1966. The army had earlier clashed with *Anya-Nya* forces and lost two men. As a reprisal they allegedly raided the village of Loronyo in the middle of the night and after shootings, set it alight. Prime Minister Sadiq denied the reports, but some people began to feel that a mutinous army had been let loose on the South by frightened officers.[36] In February 1967 at least twenty-two chiefs and tribal leaders of Bor district in Upper Nile were reported to have been killed.[37]

In a courageous and significant editorial in his newspaper, *El Hayam*, on 8 March 1967, Beshir Mohamed Said, then President of the Sudan Press Association and Director of El Hayam Press Company, demanded a thorough, high-level government inquiry into the Bor incident, where, according to the Minister of the Interior, only four tribal leaders had been killed although news reports put the death toll at twenty-three. The incident, wrote Mr Beshir, cast dark shadows over the name of the security forces in the Sudan. People in the Southern provinces now lived in terror from the rebellion and rebels on one hand, and from the security forces on the other. As was well-known, the terror caused by the security forces had had very serious effects on relations between South and North.

Among the many deplorable incidents which had happened in the South over the past two years was that of Juba, whose material and moral effects still remained, of Wau where tens of citizens had been killed, of Torit and Bor. Mr Said found it regrettable that these gruesome events had not appeared to touch the government. If the Sudanese thought that the general lack of concern and interest was helping to unify the country, then in his opinion they were a 'nation of sheep'.

Giving another side, *El Hayam* in January 1967, had published an article[38] by a Northern Sudanese living in the South, who alleged that on 2 November 1966, the rebels attacked Ghorima village, four miles from Kapoeta, killing three men and three women, and burned some huts. In December the rebels had reportedly attacked the hospital at Rumbek. On the Rumbek–Meridi road, they had attacked a Jur village and killed about twenty people. On 21 January 1967, they had attacked a police car at the Mboro police post and killed seven policemen and four civilians and wounded two policemen and a child. At the end of January the rebels had set a number of houses in Aweil town on fire. On 1 February, they had arrested two men and cut off their ears. In December, they kidnapped a chief and a court president at Wau, and so on and so forth.

On 5 May 1968, an event occurred which for many Southerners[39] symbolised North–South relations in the Sudan—the killing of William Deng (Nhial), President of SANU.[40] Mr Deng, remembered as a Southern patriot, had at one time shocked fellow nationalist leaders by advocating some form of accommodation with the North at a time when militancy was the only reputable course. According to Radio Omdurman, he was killed by 'outlaws'. But Southerners continue to state adamantly that he was murdered—along with six of his supporters—in an ambush by government forces.

Francis Mading Deng is a son of the Paramount Chief of the Ngok Dinka. He received his bachelor of law degree at Khartoum University in 1962, and his master of law and doctor of law from Yale University. He has been adjunct professor of law and anthropology at New York University. He is a member of the Human Rights Commission of the United Nations and is the author of an important book, *Tradition and Modernisation—a challenge for law among the Dinka of the Sudan* (Yale, 1971). In an interview,[41] Dr Deng once described a visit in 1970 to his home (which is in one of the Northern provinces although all the Dinka belong to one basic Negroid culture), after his father's death. There he found a frightened people. The local officer had been filling in the vacuum of Dr Deng's father's absence with many arrests, tortures and the occasional

killing. He had shot people whom he suspected of rebelliou
activities. Dr Deng's brother, who had been trying to assum(
his dead father's position, had got into great trouble and hac
finally been assassinated, together with five other members o
the family. The case was being taken seriously by the govern
ment, Dr Deng added.

The Deng family were only one of many Dinka familie
who perished in the clash of cultures. It was only after I hac
talked to African exiles and refugees from the Sudan that the
horror of the civil war was brought home to me in a persona
way. Almost every Southerner I met had lost someone in hi
family.

There were the three Sudanese students I met in Uganda
Samuel told me how, in 1962, all the 200 boys at his school i
Tonj (sixty-three miles from Rumbek) went on strike over ba(
food. Thirty of the boys were arrested, lashed and imprisoned
The Southern teachers advised the other boys, including
Samuel, to flee. In February 1966, Samuel's home at Abir
village, twenty miles from Rumbek, was among four house
burned by about thirty Northern soldiers because villager
were suspected of aiding the *Anya-Nya*. He was among
students who returned to the village and saw the burned an(
charred bodies. Two of his uncles were so charred, he told m(
that it was impossible to determine how they had died.

Marcello said he and other students fled from the village o
Opari, near Nimule, after a military camp had been am
bushed by *Anya-Nya* in June 1965. One of the few who di
not flee was a man with a broken back. He was killed on hi
sick-bed.

Charles told me how troops came to his village in Easter
Equatoria to arrest an *Anya-Nya* man. They killed the ma
and the man's mother who had harboured him, then loote(
the village.

A highly placed Southern churchman, whose sincerity wa
evident, described to me in detail how, in June 1965, he ha
been hunted by soldiers with guns at Mundri, following
dream that soldiers in a lorry were trying to kill him. Concea

ing himself behind a hedge, he saw men breaking down the doors of his house and burning down houses and other buildings in their search for him, 'and they ceremoniously shot bullets into a bible and a concordance'. This churchman told me, among other things, how, at Lui on 11 July 1965, troops killed an informer who used to give them information—then opened his pregnant wife's womb with a knife and left her and her new-born baby to bleed to death. The churchman said he had checked this story with a number of independent sources. Another Southerner—a man who impressed me with his moderation and deep knowledge of the Sudan and who has many personal friends in the North—shocked me when he said that there was more danger of under-stating than over-stating the situation in the South. In his view, most Southern sources were reliable about atrocities. He confirmed that the hot chilli torture was prevalent in the Abboud regime and said that other tortures included plucking people's nails and eyes out. He told me that many people had been so mutilated that in some cases Northern soldiers had had to kill them, whether they had found them innocent or not, because they were so disfigured. And this was from a man who time and again had emphasised that the only solution for the Sudan was for North and South to strive for reconciliation.

Certain types of atrocity stories are circulated in the wake of every war. But when General Lagu says that the hands of three Southern school children were reported to have been cut off and gives the month, the year and the area[42]—or when one reads reports of Northern men, women and children having been skinned and hung on trees by Southerners in the 1955 disturbances[43]—one hesitates to say that these things could not have happened. The world has learned the bitter fact that in this advanced century and even among the supposedly most advanced nations, excesses which seem almost unbelievable have been known to happen in times and in areas of upheaval. It is not easy, even now, to sort out the truths of the Sudan war from the half-truths and the distortions. But when one has made allowances for all the errors

E

which can occur in reports of excesses from either side due to
propaganda motivations, emotionalism, or the fact that so
much of the evidence comes, necessarily, from secondary
sources, there can still be little doubt in the mind of a reasonable observer that the record of violence in the Sixteen Years'
War was a shocking one.

There is no reason, however, to assume that no Southerners
showed mercy and kindness to Northern civilians in the South
during the 1955 uprising or that there were not some Northerners who had humane feelings for, and acted with kindness
towards, Southerners, even in the periods of greatest bitterness. From 1958 to 1967, the Governor of Upper Nile province,
Abbas Fagir, remained a pro-Southerner and it is widely
believed among Southerners that it was the Governor's close
relationship with his military counterpart in the province that
accounted in great measure for the lack of army brutality in
the province. Fagir was clearly appalled by tactics in Equatoria.[44]

He was not the only Northerner to think this way. Throughout the whole of Abboud's military government there remained such pockets of objectivity within the South. Some of
the civilian administration were clearly disgusted by the
tactics of the army men above them, and it was still possible
for Southern courts summarily to dismiss some of the more
preposterous charges against missions or Southerners.[45]

There is also little doubt that disease and privation took at
least as great a toll of Southern lives as the soldiers' bullets.
How many hospitals and other medical units were deliberately
destroyed, how much deliberate obstruction there was of
people trying to save lives and prevent the spread of disease in
the war-torn areas is still an open question. I have heard and
read many shocking reports by people who seemed to me to be
sincere and there have always been denials from the other
side. What is apparent is that often there was a complete
breakdown of co-operation in health services and that this had
appalling consequences in the areas outside government control. With the cease-fire in March 1972, the emphasis shifted

from the question of who was to blame to the problems of ensuring that there could be no recurrence of such evils.

All this serves to show how immense were the problems which the leaderships on both sides faced when they decided to end the strife and make a fresh start.

Notes to this chapter are on page 176

CHAPTER FIVE

The View from the North

Northerners generally feel that they, their policies and their problems have been misunderstood by the outside world. They say that outside criticism was often based on inadequate knowledge and distortions. This is a familiar complaint from governments everywhere, but in Khartoum it was not confined to government sources. The Northern Sudanese were highly critical of the way events in the South were often reported by western and other foreign observers. For years this was a sensitive subject particularly among intellectuals in the Northern Sudan. Perhaps the feeling that the war in the South tended to estrange and isolate the Sudan from African and other nations helped to hasten the new search for a solution in late 1971.

Since the beginning of the Long War in 1955, there had been two schools of thought in Khartoum on the Southern problem. One, represented by the Abboud regime and the Mahgoub regimes in particular, took the line that the only way to counter the force of rebellion was by counter-force. This school of thought found itself less than sympathetic to Southern grievances and aspirations. The other outlook was represented by the Sirr el Khatim caretaker government, the Nimery government (particularly in its second phase after the July 1971 upheaval) and, to a lesser degree, by the Sadiq government. It could be reduced to the simple proposition that Southerners should be won over, where possible, rather than be kept down, and hence the often-repeated declaration that the South required a political rather than a military solution. The difficulty was the discrepancy between theory and practice.

At least some Northerners not only recognised the difficulty but admitted it openly. Among those who have spoken bluntly about Northern mistakes in the South are Mohamed Omer Beshir and Beshir Mohamed Said. And neither of these two gentlemen could be accused of any lack of sympathy with the Northern position. In an interview in Khartoum on 23 December 1971, Mr Omar el Hag Mousa, Minister of Information and former brigadier in the Sudanese army, said to me: 'The Southerners were cheated for fifteen years. It is fair that some of them do not trust us. We must do things that will make them believe in us.'

But, said Beshir Mohamed Said in a book which anyone who wants to understand the philosophy and psychology of the Northern Sudanese should make a point of reading, 'it is not enough to be angry with the North and because of that go to the extreme of favouring either federation or separation'.[1] The book was published in 1965; much of what Mr Said said then is still timely today.[2]

The Northerners' case, as put by Beshir Mohamed Said, goes back to the days of slavery.[3] 'Our forefathers were slave raiders and the South was their hunting ground.' But, he insists, they were not the only people to deal in slaves. The British had done so, too, and the Italians, the Americans, the Spaniards, the Portuguese and so on. In fact, who hadn't? That did not of course alter the fact that Northern Sudanese should not have done such a thing, but times had changed and the present generation of Northerners were determined to make good the mistakes of their forefathers by helping their Southern countrymen towards progress. Their awareness of past wrong-doings would not be confined to words but would also take the form of material assistance.[4]

With the turn of the century, a new chapter started in Sudan's history. As Mr Said points out, for all practical purposes the Sudan was under British control for fifty-three years and the British must therefore take a share of the blame for Sudan's problems and of the rewards for its progress.

For over fifty years, the Southern provinces had been closed to Northerners and, for the greater part of that period, everything had been done to keep the two peoples apart. Until 1945 the policy had been to build up in the Southern Sudan a series of self-contained racial or tribal units. A firm barrier to Arabicisation had been created. Every effort had been made to establish English as the means of communication among Southerners, to the complete exclusion of Arabic.[5] Moslems among Southern officials had been dismissed, the Arabic names which some Southerners had adopted were not recognised and the wearing of Northern dress was discouraged. The memories of old hostilities were constantly revived and kept alive. As a result of this policy, Northern influence had been completely eliminated and the three Southern provinces had become a separate unit, closed to Northern Sudanese and open to others. At the same time, very little, if anything, was done to educate or raise the standards of the people in the South. Hence, he concluded, the large differences between North and South, the mistrust and the present state of misunderstanding.[6]

On the positive side Beshir Mohamed Said sees December 1946 as a milestone in British policy for the Southern part of the Sudan.[7] With the old Southern policy (1930) of dividing the South from the North replaced by a new policy (1946) designed to promote partnership between the two, the British officials who served in the Sudan in the 1940s were different from the colleagues who preceded them. Some of the old administrators had been arrogant and overwhelmed with the desire to serve, not the Sudan, but the British Empire. Former generations of Sudanese had often been uneducated and to some degree submissive. With education and experience, things changed on both sides. The British administrators became more tolerant and the Sudanese more alive to their responsibilities. In Mr Said's view, Sudan had special reason to feel grateful to Sir James Robertson, as architect of the policy that led a united Sudan to independence. He had gone ahead with his policy in the face of very strong and unfair opposition from many influential quarters.[8]

It was Sir James Robertson who had convened a conference at Juba on 12 June 1947, to ascertain from Southern spokesmen whether or not the South wished to throw in its lot with the North and be represented in the legislative assembly then envisaged.[9] While Southerners were later to claim that their delegates at Juba had been 'bribed, blackmailed and intimidated' into saying 'Yes',[10] Beshir Mohamed Said's version—the official Northern view—is that Southern representatives at the Juba conference decided of their own free will to throw in their lot with their Northern fellow countrymen.[11]

On the controversial issue of the expulsion of foreign missionaries from the Southern Sudan in 1964, Beshir Mohamed Said takes the official Northern Arab line when he says that the expulsion decision was not caused by anti-Christian motives, as some of the expelled missionaries have claimed.[12] They were expelled, he says, because they encouraged separatism, inflated racial and religious differences, interfered in politics and, in particular, raised funds and gave food and shelter to outlaws.[13] He accuses missionaries of supporting a policy of divide-and-rule. Prior to 1964, as government agents responsible for education, they had been the tools on which British policy in the Sudan relied for its execution. When things changed, the missionaries failed to change with them.[14]

Beshir Mohamed Said concedes that the missionary societies did play a part in bringing the first beginnings of education to the South;[15] and he quotes the opinion of a former British administrator that some of the missionaries in the Sudan had been 'saints'.[16] But his contention that some missionaries conspired against the unity of the Sudan[17] and bred hatred[18] is also to be found in other Sudanese writings. *Basic Facts about the Southern Provinces of the Sudan*, published by the Central Office of Information, Khartoum, in 1964, and dealing with the period before the expulsion of the missionaries, says that the missionaries wished to continue operating 'behind an iron curtain'[19] between North and South; it says their activi-

ties and unfriendly attitude towards the North accentuated
the division between the North and South;[20] and it finds no
reason why they should continue to be given the protection
and support they enjoyed for so long under the British administration.[21] In another book, which adds to our knowledge of
Northern Sudanese thinking on the Southern problem—*The
Southern Sudan: Background to Conflict*—Mohamed Omer
Beshir sees the expulsion of the missionaries as 'a logical result
arising from the hostility of the missionaries and the nature of
an army dictatorship'.[22]

In western eyes the expulsion of the missionaries was one
of the least endearing actions performed by one of the least
progressive of Sudanese administrations. Northerners such as
Mohamed Omer Beshir and Beshir Mohamed Said are too
sensitive not to be aware of this. Why then do such men show
so little concern about so drastic a decision? The answer, I
think, is to be found not so much in what the missionaries did
or did not do (and I shall look at the case for and against them
in the next chapter) as in the fact that Northern Arabs saw
the foreign Christian missionaries in Southern Sudan as
strangers within the gate who had come to sow dissent (even
if they didn't necessarily steal the silverware). To the Northern Sudanese Arab the Sudan is one country and anyone who
tries to divide it—whatever his reasons—is an enemy. Sudanese Arabs, no matter how sophisticated they may be, hold
strong traditional feelings about hospitality to strangers and
the visitor's own obligations. This may not explain the campaign against foreign missionaries in the Abboud era which
led to their expulsion. It does explain why even Northerners
who pride themselves on their tolerance still think to this day
that there was justification for kicking out the missionaries.

As well as being the author of *Background to Conflict*,
Mohamed Omer Beshir was Secretary-General of the Round
Table Conference on the South held in Khartoum from 16 to
25 March 1965. In his book, he attaches particular significance
to the inaugural address by the Prime Minister of the 'Caretaker Government', Sirr el Khatim Khalifa. The Prime

Minister started his address by pointing out, among other things, that Sudan's Southern problem had its counterpart in many other newly independent countries. After outlining the Southern problem and its origins, he went on to say that, while there were unquestionably physical, racial and cultural differences between North and South, those most to blame for the deterioration of relations between the two parts of Sudan were the British and the missionaries. He also blamed a number of Northern politicians and soldiers in the previous military regime for adopting the wrong approach to the problem. This point of view was shared by many of the Prime Minister's fellow politicians at the conference.

Many of the Northerners attending the conference were shocked to learn that the Southerners looked on them primarily as the descendants of Arab slave traders and colonisers. By the time the conference was over, they had realised that, for the time being at least, there was little hope of an agreement being reached.[23] Some of the Southerners who had gone to the conference full of hope were later to say that they had once again been disappointed. They complained that not one of the resolutions adopted at the conference was kept.[24]

Was it worthwhile holding the conference at all? Mr Beshir says, 'Yes'. If it did nothing else, it showed Northerners for the first time just how mistrusted they were in the South. They were told—in public—about the grievances of the South and the mistakes Northerners had made when attempting to solve them. They saw for themselves how history and facts were being distorted and that they, even more than British colonial policy, were being blamed for the backwardness of the Southern provinces. The conference may have failed to achieve the objective for which it was specifically called but it did give the leaders and public in both parts of the country a much better knowledge and appreciation of the extent of the Southern problem. And there was general agreement by those attending the conference that violence would not solve the problem and was contrary to the interests of both parts, and that a political solution must and could be found.[25]

Tragic deeds were to be done in the Southern Sudan before, seven years later, a political solution was seriously to be put to the test. Although himself a Northerner, Mr Beshir was candid enough to say that, in his opinion, when police and army killed Southerners at Juba and Wau in the summer of 1965,[26] they increased the bitterness of the Southern educated class and made the Southern problem more complicated and intractable.[27] He also warned his fellow Northerners that any attempt to withdraw the proposals made at the Round Table Conference and to replace them with new proposals giving less power to the South, would be interpreted by Southerners as yet another breach of promise and consequently strengthen the hands of Southern extremists.

'The immediate task,' he writes, 'is to achieve peace in the South while keeping open the dialogue between the North and the South. The peace offensive must be pursued on all fronts, for which every possible resource must be mobilised, and help enlisted from all who are keen to see peace return and national unity built in the Sudan.'[28] These words were as pertinent in 1972 as when Mr Beshir first wrote them. And whatever the conference failed to achieve, the efforts behind the scenes by men such as Mohamed Omer Beshir to achieve a new climate of thinking between North and South should not be discounted by those trying to see the Sudan story in perspective.

What material progress was there in the South? The Central Office of Information, Khartoum, in a report[29] written during the Abboud military regime and published in 1964, talked of a new phase of development and evolution in the South, gaining momentum every year.[30] It gave figures showing how the production of cotton, cloth and cotton seed and the cultivation of coffee and tobacco cash crops had increased from 1955–6 to 1961–2 (cloth production trebling); how mechanised agriculture was developing and a fruit canning factory was being established (with the help of a Russian loan); how forestry was being developed, with the South getting the lion's share of development funds (£ (Sudanese) 438,195 out of a total for the whole country of £ (Sudanese) 869,141); how sawmills were being built, and so on. Progress in health and education was also claimed, and the introduction of railways to the South by General Abboud was talked of as a major achievement.

Government departments of information tend to wear rose-tinted spectacles but Mr Said, writing in 1965,[31] confirms that much was done between independence and 1965 to raise the deplorably low standard of living in the South. He sees the share of the South in the 1960–70 development plan as 'size-able' (with £ (Sudanese) 2 million allocated for agricultural projects). He also emphasised how much remained to be done. Mr Beshir, on the other hand, writing three years later, said that the South had hardly moved out of its subsistence economy, and lagged far behind the North. He made the point, however, that there were areas in the North as backward, or even more backward, than certain areas in the South.[32]

During my own visit to the Sudan in December 1971, most people I spoke to inside and outside the government agreed that the economic situation in the South had fallen far behind the basic requirements. A report published by the Ministry of Planning[33] in 1970 was almost brutally frank about what would have to be done in the years ahead as a result of short-comings over the previous ten years in the North as well as South. In agriculture productivity was disappointing, with yield levels 'considerably lower than other countries under the same soil and climatic conditions'. Irrigated lands were used 'irrationally'. Livestock development was 'inadequate' and veterinary services 'poorly organised'. In the Sudan as a whole, national industrial development had practically stopped.

The series of booklets put out by the Ministry for Southern Affairs in 1970 under the title *A Revolution In Action* was no less candid about the economic backwardness of the South. These reports were, on the whole, optimistic about the potential of both North and South Sudan in the years ahead. A senior member of the Nimery government[34] said that the appropriation of £ (Sudanese) 4 million for a crash development programme—covering a wide range of projects from experimental studies for growing sugar cane to the reconstruction of four missionary hospitals—was only a beginning. A senior inspector of agriculture in Equatoria province told me how, since the revolution, economic agriculture was being pushed, and spoke of a big potential for sugar, coffee, tea, tobacco, pineapples and raw oil. But I found a general agreement in Khartoum that no real economic progress was possible in the South without peace.

In an address published in May 1970, General Nimery described how 'a new educational revolution—the first attempt in the last seventy years to base the whole national school system on sound educational principles'— was being applied in the South.[35] In Juba (20 December 1971), Mr Ahmed Fadel el Sid, Assistant Under-Secretary at the Ministry of Education for the Southern Provinces, told me that the new educational ladder meant that every pupil could be educated up to his capacity to learn. The smallness of the number of pupils in the South at that date (15,000 in Equatoria, 12,000 in Bahr el Ghazal and 14,000 in Upper Nile) was due to the fact that education had broken down completely when the Abboud regime closed down all schools in the South in 1964.

One of the foremost Northern intellectuals told me in a private conversation that while General Abboud had utterly failed to solve the problem of the South in human terms, it would be wrong to describe his regime as wholly bad. The opening by Abboud of rail links from the North to Juba had done more than perhaps anything else to end the physical isolation of South from North. The Nimery regime, said this man (who was not a government spokesman), had put forward bold and courageous programmes at a time when Northerners were so tired of the Southern problem that some of them felt like 'letting the South go to hell'.

The Nimery regime, I found, had certainly gone a long way towards giving Southerners positions of responsibility. Southerners in the government included the post-coup Minister for

Southern Affairs and Vice-President of the Sudan, Mr Abel
Alier. The commissioners of all three provinces were Southerners and in Equatoria a Southerner (Reuben Mac) was
given the key post of Province Commandant of Police. Southerners were getting—by order of the government—other jobs
which were formerly reserved for Northerners. The government claimed that this was only the beginning and pointed to
these appointments as evidence of its sincere desire to give the
South a new deal.[36]

Mr Hilary Logali, Commissioner for Equatoria, told me in
his office at Juba (17 December 1971) that he had no problems
on getting money he urgently needed from Khartoum to
develop the province. According to him, President Nimery
was ready to make sacrifices in the North to push development
in the South. (An exiled Southern politician, who was no
supporter of the Nimery government, told me, in London,
that he had to agree that in this respect Nimery was undoubtedly making a real effort.) Mr Logali, who belongs to the Bari
tribe and who had been Minister of Labour in the Mahgoub
government overthrown by Nimery, was in detention for a
year after the take-over. But when I questioned him on this
he said he bore Nimery no grudge for locking him up. He
had, after all, been a minister in the previous government
and so no one knew at first whether or not he could be
trusted.

Logali's attitude and the position of responsibility entrusted
to him once out of detention represented a new phase in
Northern–Southern human relations. I visited a number of
government offices in Juba where Arab Northern and African
Southern personnel were working together (in some cases with
Southerners in the top position) and, as far as an outsider can
judge, they seemed to enjoy an easy and relaxed relationship.
The Sudanese Arabs have the habit of greeting one another
not only with handshakes but with affectionate taps on the
shoulder. Ibrahim Mohamed Shager, of the Ministry of Information, Khartoum, who accompanied me to the South (but
seemed quite happy to let me go off by myself wherever I

wanted) did this not only to Arab colleagues but to Southern
colleagues and ex-colleagues. Most of the Southerners I met in
government offices seemed to be staunch supporters of the
Nimery government, but not in a subservient way—even if
some *Anya-Nya* supporters referred to them as 'stooges'. Some
of these Southerners told me that they were working for and
co-operating with the government not because they were pro-
Northern but in order to be in a position to exert pressures
on the government to get better conditions for the South.

Outside working hours in government offices there did not
seem to be much fraternising between Northerners and
Southerners.[37] One also noticed a reserve among ordinary
Southerners which indicated that fear and suspicion (and, in
particular, dread of informers) still existed. I could also see
for myself that some Northerners—unlike my ebullient friend,
Mr Shager—still looked down on Southerners. But after the
peace agreement I saw a big improvement in human relations,
and I cannot leave this subject without mentioning Dr Farouk
Ahmed Khitam, senior medical officer of the Juba Hospital.
In a huge country where there can never be sufficient doctors
or enough medical facilities, Dr Khitam, who had received his
training in Alexandria, Egypt, worked virtually round the
clock. He was in charge of a hospital with 450 beds and 3,000
to 4,000 out-patients, and he acted as physician and obstetri-
cian as well as administrator. Dr Khitam, who had served in
thirteen hospitals, could, I was told, have had a top job at
higher pay in the relative luxury of Khartoum. But he had
stayed in the South for seven years because he believed he was
more needed there—as indeed this dedicated Arab doctor
was.

The Sudan is full of sensitivities, and the feeling that the
world press was hostile to them seemed to burn deep into the
minds of Northern spokesmen. The possibility that this
hostility had in the past been largely of Northern Sudanese
making did not make them any less unhappy about it. They
were deeply resentful of allegations that the killing of civilian
in the South was the result of deliberate government policy

and they regarded as monstrous suggestions that any Sudanese government at any time was party to a policy of 'virtual genocide'. There were times when Khartoum made it difficult for journalists to get visas to visit the country at all, let alone go to the South. But after the July 1971 coup, at any rate, the official policy towards virtually all journalists was: 'We have nothing to hide. Come and see for yourselves.' And after the peace negotiations at Addis got going, a new and far more sympathetic attitude to the Sudan was apparent in the outside world in general and the media in particular.

What nearly all Northern Sudanese Arabs have in common —and in order to understand the Sudan and its problems this must be recognised—are their loyalty to the Arab world, their identification with Arab tradition and their adherence to the Muslim faith.[38] There have been periods when the rulers in the North have attempted to achieve Islamisation of the *whole* Sudan by pressure or force—in 1960 the Abboud regime ruled that Friday must replace Sunday as a day of rest in the South. There have been other regimes, such as the Nimery admin-istration, which have put emphasis on religious toleration and during which Southerners have been freely permitted to worship as they please, refrain from work on Sundays, enjoy the Christmas celebrations and take up to four days off for Easter. But whereas the question of an Islamic constitution continued to be a contentious issue between 'moderates' and 'zealots' in the Northern Muslim fold, the Arab North has always believed that, in the interests of all sections, Arabic should be the common medium of communication in the whole country. Northerners have never been able to forget the British administrators and foreign missionaries tried to kill Arabic as a language in the South during the time of the 'Southern policy'. President Nimery believed as firmly as any other Northerner in the cultural importance of Arabic. Out-lining the details of settlement of the Sixteen Years' War, he told a Northern audience that the Southerners had agreed to the principle that Arabic was the country's official language in the basic law.[39] But, he added, 'proceeding from a con-

scious awareness of the facts and the present practical circumstances', the government had agreed that English should be a
working language in the region beside the local basic languages. In Northern eyes this was not only a gesture of goodwill
but a big concession.

Notes to this chapter are on page 178

CHAPTER SIX

The Missionaries

The Cotran commission of inquiry said in 1955 that some Northern administrators in Southern Sudan had levelled criticisms against missionary education, and that a few had even accused the missionaries of being one of the prime causes of the 1955 disturbances. The missionaries, said their accusers, had been promoting Christianity at the expense of Islam. They had labelled the Northerners as slave traders and had included the history of the slave trade in the school curriculum. They were also supposed to have written books and pamphlets on the subject, although none of these were produced as evidence before the commission. The commissioners found, however, that, although the missionaries undoubtedly regarded the influx of Northern administrators as a kind of challenge to their own authority, all the indications were that the trouble in the South was of a political rather than a religious nature.[1]

The second criticism put by Northerners to the commissioners was that missionaries were generally not equipped to teach, in as much as their educational training and general outlook were limited to the task of promoting Christianity. The commission found more substance in this criticism. When the missionaries had been in almost exclusive control of education in Southern Sudan between 1927 and 1946, they had failed, with a few notable exceptions, to produce Southern staff able or trained to assume executive or administrative positions, said the commission.[2]

The commission's conclusions apart, there is general agree-

F

ment that the war was not a religious one. A few dedicated
missionaries continued to regard it as such and to see the
threat of Islamisation as the South's major problem. But there
were many others who, in spite of their own concern with the
religious aspect, saw the war for what it was—a political conflict arising from conflicting cultural and other interests. As
one scholar of Sudanese affairs put it, it was hard to keep up
the myth of a daily struggle in the South between the Crescent
and the Cross when the Christianisation of the majority of the
people was proceeding so slowly.[3] The struggle, in many pro-
Southern eyes, was concerned with the saving of lives rather
than the saving of souls. It was a battle for human freedoms,
of which religious freedom was one. In pro-Northern eyes, it
was a fight to unify the country and maintain security.

There was—and still is to this day—a sharper division of
opinion on two of the issues which the commission's report
touched upon: (1) the quality and value of missionary education and work in the Southern Sudan; (2) the question of
the responsibility of missionaries for the hostility which led to
and prolonged the civil war. And this gave rise to another
question: did the Sudanese government of the day have any
justification for expelling all foreign Christian missionaries in
1964?

Christian missionary societies established themselves in the
Southern Sudan as early as 1848, but their more active phase
began with the British reconquest in 1898. At the beginning
of the twentieth century, the British-controlled government
allotted specific areas to the different missions in order to
avoid sectarian frictions. The United Presbyterian Church of
the United States of America began work among the Shilluk;
the Church Missionary Society (Anglican) among the Dinka;
the Roman Catholics among Dinka and Shilluk. The missionaries were entrusted with the development of education. In
addition to their religious and medical work, they established
their own schools which, until 1927, were free from government supervision and control.[4] By the late 1930s, missionaries
were widely assumed by educated Northerners to be turning

the Southern Sudanese into black Englishmen. In fact, the majority of missionaries in the South were not English but were of Italian peasant stock.[5] At the time of the expulsion there were 335 missionaries working in the South. Of these 272 were Roman Catholic—Verona Fathers and Mill Hill Fathers; and 63 were Protestants—Church Missionary Society, American Presbyterian Mission, African Inland Mission (American) and the Sudan Interior Mission. There were 231 Catholic and 51 Protestant missionaries working in the North. The 272 Catholics[6] and (according to one usually reliable Northern source[7]) 28 of the Protestants were expelled from the South. Those working in the North were allowed to continue their educational and other activities.[8]

The official line from Khartoum was that most missionaries were propagators of faith and not teachers and were therefore not the people to be entrusted with the education of the Southern Sudanese. The emphasis in education in the South had, they said, been on the very lowest stages of the educational ladder. The educational policy had been designed to arrest rather than encourage the mental and cultural development of boys and girls in their formative years—as could be seen from the fact that by 1914 only two Southern students had finished their secondary education in Uganda.[9] Another Northern source[10] quotes the Governor-General of the Sudan in 1927 as saying, following a visit to the Southern provinces, that he was very far from satisfied with the work of the missionaries in the field of education. They had, said the Governor in his report, made no real effort to seize their opportunities. They lacked vision and were hedged in by pettiness of outlook and by their bias against the social and matrimonial customs of the people. He was convinced that on their present lines, they would not perform the functions expected of them. If the government were to enter the field, it might stimulate them to justify their presence and to act more broadmindedly than they did at present. The fault of the 'sphere system', continued the Governor, was that it excluded competition and produced inefficiency and self-satisfaction.

Few Southerners I have met would quarrel with the contention that in education as in other matters the South lagged woefully behind the North. But few blamed the missionaries for this. The fault, they said, lay elsewhere. In the opinion of at least one former British administrator in the Sudan, the standard of education provided by the missions may not always have been satisfactory but, when it came to medical work and technical education, the Southerner owed a great deal to many unselfish missionaries—particularly the Roman Catholics— who spent the best part of their lives in his service.[11] If there were very few educated people in the South to take over leadership, there would have been fewer still without the mission schools; if the literacy rate was low, it would have been far lower. The fact was that for most of the British administration's time in the South, the alternative to mission education was none at all.[12]

Why, Southerners asked, did the British rulers wait till 1927 to take any real interest in—and subsidise—mission schools? Why was it not until 1946 that the government really 'got hold' of Southern education when it consolidated purely government schools with non-mission headmasters and teachers and began the effort to catch up the lost ground? A Sudanese Minister of Education,[13] a Northerner, speaking in Parliament on 11 April 1954, blamed 'the previous imperialists' and not the missionaries for the bad state of affairs in the South. It was for this reason, he said, that the Ministry of Education would not be absorbing the mission schools into its system. And a Southern Member of Parliament, Kosmas Rababa, said in the same Parliament on 26 April 1954 that, in his opinion, the Sudanese government should be grateful to the missionaries. For fifty years they had been the only source of education for Southerners. Without them, there would have been no Southerners in Parliament at all.[14]

When the mission schools were nationalised in 1957, the then Minister of Education[15] expressed the appreciation of his government for the 'good and devoted work' the missionaries had done in the field of Southern education since the begin-

ning of the century. He assured them that the new policy did
not in any way imply that the government looked on the
mission system of education as 'being disruptive to the national
harmony'.

What did nationalisation of the mission schools mean for
Southern children after the military takeover in 1958? According to the Southern Front,[16] the policy of the Abboud government was to give the minimum education to the minimum
number of Southern children. According to these and other
Southern sources, education in the South, far from improving,
suffered after the mission schools were closed down[17]—right
up to the time of the Nimery regime's new policy for the
South which had still to be put to the test.

In 1962 the Supreme Council of the Armed Forces promul-
gated a new Missionary Societies Act whose aim was to provide
the missions with a legal status and regulate their religious
work. The Abboud government claimed that there was no
religious discrimination in the legislation which applied to all
religions, Islam and Christianity among them. It claimed to
respect and treat them all on an equal footing 'without prejudice or favouritism'.[18] The missionaries, however, pointed out
that under the act they were forbidden to preach, baptise,
perform any kind of missionary work, aid orphans, train
seminarians and the members of religious societies, organise
social and recreational facilities, play records and show films
to people, distribute religious publications, have buildings
repaired and perform work of charity, without first obtaining
the permission of the Council of Ministers.[19] The missionaries
saw this act as hastening the end of their work in the Southern
Sudan; and two years later all foreign missionaries were
expelled from the South.

In 1955 the Cotran commission had thrown out of court the
allegation that missionaries were to blame for the Equatoria
uprising; and in 1963 a Northern Sudanese court dismissed as
baseless an army charge that five Roman Catholic priests were
behind a raid on Wau, even though the Catholics have already
focussed much international publicity on Christian persecu-

tion.[20] But up to this day Northerners have attempted to justify the 1964 expulsions. Beshir Mohamed Said, who is widely respected for his reasonableness and tolerance on other matters, was critical in his judgement of missionaries, who, he said, had left no stone unturned to intensify the feelings of Southerners against the North. He said that there was abundant evidence that the missionaries had interfered in politics, aided outlaws and worked against the unity of Sudan. The missionaries, he claimed, had never publicly deplored the wholesale butchering of Northerners in the 1955 mutiny. They had never told their audience in church, school or market that it was wrong to kill Northerners. And, while there was no direct evidence that they were behind the mutiny, everyone knew that to keep silent about a crime was much the same as taking part in it oneself.[21]

The expulsion of the missionaries shocked the Christian world. I personally share the view that it was unjustifiable and harmful to all concerned. A government which was intent on Islamisation had reason to regard the Christian missionaries as competitors and even enemies. But the accusation that the missionaries in general interfered in politics, ignored the laws of the land and encouraged Southerners to break the law was, I believe, no more borne out by facts than the allegations which a government-appointed Sudanese commission of inquiry[22] had dismissed as baseless nine years previously.

A memorandum giving the reasons behind the expulsion of foreign missionaries and priests from the Southern provinces was published by the Ministry of the Interior, Khartoum, on 5 March 1964 in Arabic and English. In it, the government claimed that all the allegations made against the missionaries had been 'proved beyond doubt'.[23] At Verona, on 5 August, of the same year, Catholic missionaries expelled from the Southern Sudan put out a book, *The Black Book of the Sudan: an Answer*, which examined and refuted the allegations and statements made in the memorandum, point by point.

The government had claimed that the missionaries had acted as British agents in colonial times. Not true, replied the missionaries. As others had already pointed out,[24] the charge was almost laughable seeing that most of the missionaries in the South were not British but Italian Catholics.

Khartoum's accusation that they had joined with the British in encouraging the creation of a separate identity for the South was equally untrue. In fact the arrival of Christianity and the missions had had a salutary effect on Southern passions. Traditional tribal feuding started to die out and, in the years before independence, Southern mistrust and hatred for the Northerners were definitely waning. Then came independence and the Southerners quickly realised that the Northerners had not made equal progress towards greater respect for one's fellow countrymen.

Khartoum had said that the missionaries intentionally stirred up national aspirations and sentiments based on fear, hate and distrust of the Northerners. An independent commission of inquiry had already found this charge baseless in 1955. Any fear felt by Southerners was not the missions' doing.

The accusation that they had tried to make the North and South as different from each other as possible was also without foundation. Everyone knew that missionaries worked in North Sudan as well as in the South and that the missions were open to every Sudanese, whether Northerner or Southerner.

According to Khartoum, they had encouraged the separatist movement in the South. Their reply was that politics was not part of a missionary's work. There were only a scattered number of missionaries to attend to the spiritual needs of thousands. Even if missionaries had had the inclination to mix in politics, they would not have had the time.

Khartoum's statement that a missionary should confine his activities to religion alone was based on a misunderstanding. A Christian missionary's role was not the same as that of an Imam. He traditionally had pastoral and social duties as well as religious ones. He would obey with a heavy heart if the Sudanese government forbade him to carry these out. But when his everyday activities as a missionary were dubbed as political manipulation for subversive ends, he demanded that these accusations should be proved clearly, cases by case.

Khartoum had condemned the missionaries for their lack of teaching skill. Why then had a Minister of Education[25] publicly praised them in the Sudanese Parliament in 1954 for their 'good and devoted work in Southern education'?

Finally, they had been accused by the Minister of Information[26] in February 1964, of having been involved in provoking incidents in which Northerners were killed in the South in 1955. They challenged the government to quote one instance in the report of the commission of inquiry into the 1955 disturbances where a missionary had been proved to have been implicated in the death of a Northerner.[27]

In vindication of the wholesale expulsions, the memorandum gave details of cases in which missionaries were alleged to have committed political crimes and to have given support to outlaws. The evidence presented in *The Black Book* indicates the harassment of missionaries by the Abboud regime rather than any kind of conspiracy by missionaries against the government. For many of these dedicated people, forced removal from the country, the people and the work they loved was like a separation between parents and children. Some of them continued in exile to work for their beloved South. The nature of these activities in exile led to differences of opinion inside, as well as outside, the Church. In an interview with Per Oyvind Heradstveit, of the Norwegian Broadcasting Corporation, in Khartoum on 20 August 1970, Mohamed Omer Beshir (then head of the African department of the Foreign Ministry) expressed the view—widely held in the North—that some of the aid given to Southerners by church organisations was sold and turned into arms. He said he also thought that the Verona Fathers were giving aid to the rebels for political reasons, and added: 'I don't personally have the proof but I think the Sudan government has the proof.' I personally have no doubt, as a result of my own investigations, that whatever aid these and other church organisations gave to the South, the motivation was on the whole humanitarian and idealistic.

In the absence of the foreign missionary leaders, African Sudanese churchmen in the South continued missionary work —often under great difficulties. It should be emphasised that the principal missions in the South were branches of their Northern headquarters and even among missionaries who were obsessed with the idea of the 'Muslim menace', the job was not to convert Muslims (Muslims still attend Christian schools in the North but take their own religious instruction) but to bring pagans to Christianity. It is apparent that a slow but steady Christianisation continued in spite of the obstacles.[28]

The Nimery administration's new liberalising policy after the July 1971 counter-coup brought with it evident signs of greater religious freedom, fewer restrictions and more facilities for Christian church workers in both parts of the country. It was also evident that in the religious as well as other fields of activity in the South, the trend would be to encourage Southern leadership.

Notes to this chapter are on page 180

CHAPTER SEVEN

The Rise of the Anya-Nya

Southern politicians may be said to have had a preliminary blooding at the Juba Conference, called by the Civil Secretary, Sir James Robertson, on 12 June 1947, and attended by fifteen Southerners (chosen by the Governors of the Southern provinces), six British officials and six Northerners. What precisely was decided at the conference remains an historical controversy—Northerners insisting that the Southern representatives agreed to political unity with the North; and Southerners claiming that they had agreed, with great reluctance, to participate with the far more politically experienced Northerners in a Legislative Assembly only because they had been warned that otherwise they would have no say at all in the future government of the Sudan.

The Legislative Assembly opened on 23 December 1948 with 13 nominated members for the South (a shock because Southerners claimed that they had been promised there would be at least 15 Southern members drawn from Provincial Councils[1]) as against 76 for the North and 6 British. Mr Buth Diu, the only Southern member to be represented on the Constitution Committee—appointed on 26 March 1961 to recommend steps to be taken for the granting to the Sudan of self-government—resigned from the committee when the Southern proposal for federal status was rejected. Along with Stanislaus Paysama and Abdel Rahman Sule (a Muslim thereafter known as 'The Patron'), Buth Diu, in the same year, founded the South's first political movement; and it was officially registered two years later as the Southern Party. In the October 1953 elections, in which the South was given 22 out of 97 seats, the Southern Party (as mentioned in Chapter 1) won 16; and the National Unionist Party (NUP), which won an overwhelming victory in the North, got the remaining 6 in the South. When in 1954 the Southern Party was renamed the Liberal Party, Mr Paysama became President and Mr Buth Diu (a Nuer who had once been a houseboy and had no formal education) became Secretary-General. The Liberal Party made such headway that, when it called on all Southern members of Parliament to form a Southern Bloc to pursue Southern demands for federation, two Southern members of the NUP who were ministers in Mr Ismail el Azhari's government crossed over to the Liberal Party.

But the party, feeling its way in the strange, new world of political contest, developed internal dissensions. Buth Diu, an ambitious man whose subsequent political career was to make him a controversial figure, decided to identify himself with the government party[2] after his name had appeared—apparently without justification[3]—in an implicating document in connection with the 1955 disturbances. Paysama, who came originally from the Northern ('Negro') province of Darfur, contested the presidency with Benjamin Lwoki, a Kakwa from Yei in the South. In the general elections which ended on 8 March 1958, Lwoki and many of his supporters lost their parliamentary seats. The wing led by Paysama was successful, and Paysama formed a Southern Bloc which won the majority of the South's by then forty-six seats. Father Saturnino Lohure, a Catholic priest who had stood as an Independent, was elected President of the Bloc[4] and Luigi Adwok, a school teacher and son of a Shilluk chief, was elected Secretary-General. (Ezbon Mondiri, who in 1957 had founded a 'Federal Party', was among those elected to Parliament but was given a prison sentence on charges of inciting hatred against the government and the North.[5]) Both Saturnino and Adwok resigned from their posts in the Bloc and were succeeded respectively by Elijah A. Mayom and Franco W. Garang (elder brother of Joseph U. Garang, who was later executed). With the banning of political parties and the dissolution of Parliament after General Abboud's takeover in November 1958, the struggle within a struggle continued for Southern politicians underground and in exile.

Father Saturnino, Joseph Oduho and William Deng (who was at the time Acting District Commissioner for the Sudan Government in Kapoeta) were among those who fled from the Sudan after the discovery of an alleged plot to arrest Southern politicians on Christmas Eve 1960.[6] As refugees at Leopoldville (now Kinshasa) these three in February 1962 founded a movement in exile called the Sudan African Closed Districts National Union (SACDNU). Oduho became President, Deng Secretary-General, and Aggrey Jaden Deputy Secretary-General. In 1963 the name of the movement was changed to the simpler SANU (Sudan African National Union), with headquarters at Kampala.

With the return of civilian government to the Sudan in 1964, the Southern Front was formed, headed by Southern intellectuals and civil servants. The Southern Front had its headquarters in Khartoum and it provided three ministers in the caretaker government of Sirr el Khatim: Clement Mboro, who had participated in the 1947 Juba Conference and who was later to become the acknowledged leader of the South, became Minister of the Interior; Hilary Paul Logali, an intelligent and astute Protestant from the Bari tribe, became Minister of Works; and Ezbon Mondiri (released from prison) became Minister of Communications (he was later replaced by Gordon Muortat Mayen). In June 1965 the Southern Front became a formally registered political party, with Clement Mboro as President, Gordon Muortat Mayen as Vice-President and Hilary Paul Logali as Secretary-General. Before that the caretaker government, on the recommendation of the Southern Front, had invited representatives of all Southern groups to attend a round table conference. The Southern Fronters at first supported the demand by leaders in exile that the talks be held outside the Sudan but when difficulties arose over this they agreed to an invitation to attend the talks in Khartoum.

SANU split over this and other matters. At a convention held in Kampala in November 1964, Aggrey Jaden succeeded Joseph Oduho as President of SANU and Philip Pedak became Vice-President. William Deng stayed away from the convention and on his own initiative declared to the Sudan government that he, as the representative of SANU, would come to Khartoum for the round table conference. Eventually the Southern Front persuaded the new executive of SANU to attend and to allow William Deng to be a SANU delegate. When the conference opened on 16 March 1965, SANU maintained that in Aggrey Jaden's absence Elia Lupe (Baraba) would be their leader. But William Deng persisted in referring to himself as the leader of the delegation. When the conference ended, Deng remained and founded a new party which he also called SANU-inside-the-Sudan, and declared that SANU-outside had ceased to exist.

It was a time of much confusion. In June 1965, in East Africa, Joseph Oduho, Father Saturnino and others broke away from SANU-in-exile and formed a new grouping called the Azania[7] Liberation Front (ALF). Aggrey Jaden then organised another new organisation which he named the Sudan African Liberation Front (SALF). The two groups merged later that year to become ALF—with Oduho President and Jaden Vice-President. Still another offshoot of the original SANU-in-exile called itself the Sudan African Union of Conservatives and also became known as Sudan African Freedom Fighters' Union of Conservatives (a mouthful abbreviated into SAFFUC), but it had little mass appeal and disappeared into obscurity. Meanwhile, inside the Sudan, to add to the welter of political confusion, two other small Southern parties had been started up early in 1965: the old Liberal Party revived by veterans Stanislaus Paysama and Buth Diu; and the Sudan United Party, founded by Santino Deng. It is difficult for any Southerner to write objectively about these matters particularly if he has been as closely involved as was Oliver Albino, author of *The Sudan: a Southern Viewpoint*. But Santino Deng was the sole Southern minister during the

Abboud regime when other Southern leaders refused to have
dealings with it; and Mr Álbino's description of him as a man
who had 'completely lost the confidence of the Southern
people'[8] does not seem unduly harsh. According to Albino,
the two parties remained too small to be taken seriously; and
he cites a third, the Southern Peace Party, which he dismisses
as a mere front organisation for certain Northern politicians.[9]

Meanwhile in June 1965—a fateful month in Sudanese
politics—a new government had come in under Mohamed
Ahmad Mahgoub; the Southern Front pulled out of government, leaving the South represented at ministerial level only
by two SANU-inside (pre-SALF) men; and when they withdrew in protest against the appointment of Buth Diu as
Minister of Animal Resources, the imperturbable Mr Buth
Diu remained sole Southern representative in the Cabinet
until 1966 when one of the first actions of the new Premier,
Sadiq el Mahdi, was to remove Diu and replace him by two
civil servants. In January 1967 the South mourned the death
of Father Saturnino, one of its unquestionably respected
leaders.

Throughout the period (except for a brief time in 1964
when Father Saturnino, Joseph Oduho, Aggrey Jaden, William Deng and Clement Mboro appeared to be in harness
together) Northern politicians were able to exploit the frag-
mentation of the Southern political movement. In August
1967, Gordon Muortat Mayen, Archangelo Barri Wanji and
Elia Lupe, a former MP who had been one of the first
Southern police officers, organised—with others—the famous
Angrudi Convention in Eastern Equatoria where, at a large
convention of Southerners in the liberation movement, a
decision was made to replace all 'liberation' parties by a single
party called the 'Southern Sudan Provisional Government'
(SSPG). But two of the Southern parties—the Southern Front
and William Deng's SANU—continued to function and each
won some seats in the 1968 elections. Meanwhile a split developed between Jaden (a Bari), who had become President
of the SSPG, and Mayen and his so-called 'Dinka clique'.[10]

The SSPG broke down under the weight of tribal and other divisions; and in March 1969 it was replaced by the 'Nile Provisional Government' (NPG) with Mayen as President and Marco Rume as Vice-President. The Nile Provisional Government then also proceeded to split. Emilio Tafeng, at that time Commander-in-Chief of the *Anya-Nya*, became engaged in a struggle with Mayen for the leadership of the NPG and then went off—with his Chief of Staff, Fredrick Maggott, a former captain in the Sudanese army—to form a splinter movement, the 'Anidi Revolutionary Government'. In the West, along the Congo border, former MP Michael Tawili announced the creation of a Zande separatist movement—which he called the 'Sue River Revolutionary Government' (it was also known as the 'Suer Republic'). In 1970 they all broke up and the Southern Sudan Liberation Movement was formed, with the *Anya-Nya* as its military wing. At last there was a more or less cohesive force in the South which continued to function as such until Southern resistance ceased by agreement in 1972.

There are differing views on when the war began. I personally subscribe to the view that it opened in 1955—because from the time the Southern Corps mutinied in Equatoria in August of that year until the cease-fire in 1972 the South knew no peace. The resistance movement, which was ultimately to come under the unifying control of General Joseph Lagu, had its beginnings when at the close of the mutiny some elements of the Equatoria Corps fled into the bush to avoid reprisals. In spite of assurances that mutineers who surrendered would not be punished, those who remained were victimised (according to every South report I have come across), many being shot. Reprisals by the Northern army—which were only to be expected in view of the excesses committed by Southerners against Northerners during the 1955 disturbances[11]—continued sporadically for a long time; and the struggle, if intermittent, was ferocious. Independence for the Sudan came in January 1956 amidst what some Southerners have described as a reign of terror for the South.[12]

With the advent of the Abboud military regime in 1958

and a new programme of repressive control in the South under the direction of Ali Baldo, Governor of Equatoria (a name
which struck terror into many Southern hearts), more and
more Southerners fled—some to cross the border as refugees,
others to join the 'bandits' in the bush, Many of the schoolboys called out on strike by William Deng in 1962 in protest
against cruel treatment and discrimination by Arab teachers
were to become soldiers in the new 'liberation' army (in
Southern eyes they were 'freedom fighters'; in Northern eyes
'bandits'). By September 1963 the recruits had swelled into
thousands. The second phase of resistance had begun—on a
new, large scale. The name that burned deep into the unfold-
ing chapter of resistance was Pacalla.

Pacalla was a government post in the Upper Nile province;
and it was the first—according to the records—to be captured
by the rebels, who by this time had organised themselves under the name of *Anya-Nya*. It was, by all accounts, a brutal
business. After a three-day battle, shops, prison and police
lines all fell to the rebels, who killed all the Northern traders
except for one woman. After a week the *Anya-Nya* evacuated
Pacalla. In the same month (September 1963) the *Anya-Nya*
opened an offensive in Equatoria, where the police post of
Kajo-Kaji, near the Uganda border, was captured and several
Northern policemen killed. On 11 January 1964 a rebel force
under Bernandino Mau, the son of a Dinka chief, in Bahr el
Ghazal, attempted to capture the town of Wau and its
armoury but the rebels were driven off and Mau and two
others were hanged.

The *Anya-Nya* at first were armed with only spears,
machettes and bows and arrows, apart from the few guns they
captured from Northerners. But in 1965 the whole com-
plexion of their campaign altered when they came into possession of quantities of arms which had originally been
transported, with Khartoum's help, from Algeria and Egypt
through the Southern Sudan to the Congolese Simbas. These
arms were then either abandoned by the rebel Simbas, following the defeat of their revolt against the Tschombe govern-

ment, or were sold by them for food as they fled across the border into the Sudan. More and more the *Anya-Nya* began to gain control of the countryside (although the extent of that control is contested by Northern sources) while the towns remained under government control.

The rebels acquired a reputation for both strengths and weaknesses, and legends sprang up around them. Their very name, *Anya-Nya*, was a legend—it was said to be a Lotuko version of the term *Inya-Nya*, which in the Madi and Moru languages means literally 'the venom of the Gabon viper'; and they were credited with the emblem of a charging buffalo surrounded by two cobras, the whole split by an arrow (the significance being the buffalo bull's might and the deadliness of a snake). Some of the small number of journalists who managed to visit *Anya-Nya* territory clandestinely outdid one another in vivid descriptions. And so an astonished (but generally unconcerned) world was told of an officer in tattered trousers drilling soldiers looking vastly more military than himself; of forty-miles-a-day marches through rough, unyielding country; of 'Goliaths handling heavy Brens like popguns'; of soldiers who seemed to have renounced women in their dedication to their fight;[13] of an army that 'fights on a diet of crocodiles' and used dug-out canoes for transport.[14] And I have no doubt it was all true.

The weaknesses attributed in the early years to the *Anya-Nya* movement (in reports by observers) were many. They were said to include the smallness of the educated elite; lack of discipline; personal misuse of money; poor sense of organisation; poor time sense; little combat experience; poverty; inferior military equipment; shortage of external sources of supply; lack of support from neighbouring African countries; no developed resources to sell in return for foreign backing; an extremely high death rate from disease; poor to nonexistent communications and transport; lack of knowledge of the techniques used by other guerilla movements. ('This is certainly a hell of a list,' one commentator observed, 'and in places other than the Sudan might have proved fatal.')

G

There were the handicaps of tribalism and tribal differences.
A Southern friend told me that the *Anya-Nya* had, for a long
time, been a disorganised movement, based on the whims of
individual groups, each fighting in its own tribal area. There
was also the story, said to have emanated from the West German mercenary, Rolf Steiner, of carefully planned attacks on
an army position ending in confusion with one or other of
the resistance platoons deciding to fight its own private war,
losing its way or not fighting at all. One reporter, who spent
several months with the rebels, said that after several months
of training many of the men used to run away with their arms,
preferring to soldier in their own tribal areas under local self-
appointed colonels.[15]

How much of this was fair and accurate judgement? (Steiner
—who attached himself to General Tafeng but was disowned
by the *Anya-Nya* High Command—is suspect.[16]) To some extent these and other impressions could have been based on
outsiders' conceptions of what African guerilla movements
are like, or on over-critical assessments in necessarily confused situations. It was inevitable, however, that, in a guerilla
force operating over so large a terrain, individual units would
tend to act independently of, and sometimes at variance with,
one another; that morale and discipline would vary; that the
individual commanders, representing a variety of tribal
affiliations, would have disputes through sheer clash of personalities or quarrel over the supply of sorely needed
weapons.[17]

But the weaknesses began to recede and the strengths to
manifest themselves when General Joseph Lagu succeeded
in bringing all military resistance under a more or less unified
command. The strengths included the courage and resource-
fulness of the resistance fighters, their sense of dedication and
the fact that they had a continuing supply of natural leaders.
They were fighting in terrain which gave them great advantage for a cause about which few had any doubts. Not least of
all these was the quality of General Lagu's own leadership.
His grip tightened. He was, above all, the man who had sole

access to arms supplies; and under his leadership there was a notable tightening up of discipline and a measure of inter-tribal unity was apparent at least during that time.

Lagu's organisation was re-formed as the Southern Sudan Liberation Front, with *Anya-Nya* as its military wing. He called together the various Southern political leaders to form a political wing of the Front; and by 1971 Major-General Joseph Lagu, in addition to being Commander-in-Chief of the *Anya-Nya* armed forces, was undisputed leader of the Southern Sudan Liberation Movement. In order to get the military machine functioning more smoothly Lagu had to make certain changes in command.[18] Towards the end of January 1972, during discussions I had with him in East Africa, General Lagu wrote out for me the 'Governing Authority';

HIGH COMMAND
Major-General Joseph Lagu, C-in-C
Brigadier Joseph Akuon, CO 2nd Brigade, Upper Nile[19]
Col Fredrick Maggott, CO 1st Brigade, Equatoria
Col Emmanuel Abur, SO 3rd Brigade, Bahr el Ghazal

HIGH CIVIL AUTHORITY
Mr Elia Lupe, Chief Commissioner
Mr Elisapana Mulla, Commissioner of Equatoria
Mr Antipas Ayiei, Commissioner for Upper Nile
Mr Dishan Ojwe, Police Commissioner
Commissioner for Bahr el Ghazal—vacant

EMISSARIES
Mading de Garang—London
Lawrence Wol Wol—Paris
Dominic Mohamed—Washington
Angelo Voga—East Africa (Kampala)
Job Adier—Addis Ababa

The *Anya-Nya* were always greatly out-weaponed by General Nimery's army. They were almost certainly out-

numbered too: the guerrilla force at the end of 1971 was
variously estimated at anything between 5,000 and 40,000
men. Sources close to the *Anya-Nya* put it at 12,000 full-
timers with thousands more part-timers or reserves. Major-
General Gadir, then Chief of Staff of the Sudanese army, told
me in December 1971 that he estimated the *Anya-Nya*
strength at 10,000—a third of it fully armed.

As a guerrilla force, it asked for no quarter and gave no
quarter. Few prisoners were taken by either side. As was to
be expected, there were conflicting reports about the guerrilla
force's relations with Southern civilians. In the days before
Lagu's unified leadership the ordinary people in the countryside were evidently in fear of both the guerrillas and the
Northern troops. If they co-operated with the *Anya-Nya* by
giving them food and shelter and paying taxes to them, they
ran the risk of being shot by the government forces; and
Southern sources insist that tens of thousands of Southerners
were killed for this reason or even when they were suspected
of giving such aid. But if they refused to aid the guerrillas or
co-operated with government, they ran the risk of reprisals
from the *Anya-Nya*. From what Southerners have told me
there was a measure of *Anya-Nya* brutality to Southern
civilians—particularly earlier when the guerrilla force was
divided into independent and not always well-controlled units
(see Chapter 4 for allegations made against the *Anya-Nya* in
the Sudanese newspaper, *El Hayam*). There was also a positive, non-military side to *Anya-Nya* activities, and this
attracted a number of dedicated people, Sudanese and non-
Sudanese, from inside and outside the Church, a number of
whom I met personally.

Early in 1971, Lagu himself wrote that the *Anya-Nya*
guerrilla movement had come into being in 1963–4 when it
became clear to the Southern Sudanese that, without political
power, the South could not hope to control its economic,
social and cultural development. After establishing some
security and administrative measures in the countryside, the
movement started to attend to aspects of life in the South

which up to then had been neglected. It set up, for instance, schools, so that now there were about 200 elementary schools in Juba and Yei districts alone. The movement had established cotton industries in Zandeland and, by early 1971, soap, salt and cooking oil were also being manufactured there as well.[20]

Eliaba Surur, who acted as Commissioner for Education, told me when I met him in East Africa in January 1972 that there were by then about 500 primitive schools in the bush, each containing about 200 pupils. Most of the schools were in Equatoria. There was a desperate shortage of books, paper, pencils, blackboards, etc, and children had often to write in the sand. In spite of the immense difficulties caused by lack of funds, the educational programme was being pushed ahead with the co-operation of church people. A training centre had been set up in the bush under a principal who was formerly a principal in the Sudan government. English, mathematics, geography, history, science and religion were taught. A system of organised community education was also introduced, under which literate adults made up for the shortage of trained teachers by passing on what they had learned.

In spite of comparable difficulties, medical services were set up by the Liberation Movement. A report issued on 26 February 1972 showed that there was one recognised medical centre for the training of medical personnel all over the South. Fifteen dispensaries had been set up in Eastern Equatoria under the civil administration of the Liberation Front, and two dispensaries in the central area of Western Equatoria. The other areas of the country were served by *Anya-Nya* military medical centres. The pressing problem was the shortage of drugs.

Civil organisation of a kind had its beginnings in the establishment of markets and rudimentary administration in Bari and Moru regions of Equatoria by Ezbon Mondiri in 1965. Mondiri's idea of dividing the Southern Sudan into nine regions for administrative purposes was taken up by the SSPG. Lagu's Liberation Front formed a civilian structure based on the old district commissioner system. The man primarily responsible for the development of the movement's civil administration system was Elisapana Mulla, a former Sudanese civil servant whom Lagu appointed Commissioner for Equatoria. Mulla established an *Anya-Nya* civil administration centre at Langayu (forty miles from the Uganda border) where *Anya-Nya* civil servants were trained not only in such matters as tax collection but in legal administration—based on the British system. And the British legal system was increasingly being used as a guide by tribal chiefs trying communal cases and in civil cases among the *Anya-Nya*.

Notes to this chapter are on page 181

CHAPTER EIGHT

Russians in the Sudan

One of the most controversial features of the Long War was the role played by the Soviet Union. It was generally acknowledged that aircraft and weapons used by the government forces came mainly from Russia. The extent of Soviet participation in attacks on the South was debatable. Both Moscow and Khartoum repeatedly denied any direct Russian intervention in the South. Southern sources, western and African diplomats and other observers reported variously on Soviet involvement. The evidence, largely circumstantial, mounted up.

The intense Soviet interest in the Sudan dated back to January 1968 when a hundred million dollar Sudan–Soviet agreement was reached (twelve years after diplomatic relations between the two countries were established on 17 March 1956). Before it was overthrown in May 1969 the government of Mohamed Ahmad Mahgoub concluded an arms deal with the Soviet government (Mr Mahgoub insisted in an interview with me in January 1972, in London, that the Migs and helicopters he ordered from Moscow were purely for external defence.) It was not until after the Nimery regime's takeover that Soviet influence began to be felt in the Sudan.[1] Before 1970 there were no military advisers in the country. By the time of the abortive coup against Nimery in July 1971 their numbers were variously estimated to be between 200 and 3,000. (The latter figure, from a Southern source, was said to include military instructors as well.)[2] Early in 1971, President Amin of Uganda told a press conference at Kampala that his

predecessor, Milton Obote, had accepted the presence of
Soviet military instructors in the Ugandan North, from where
they could have led a pincer movement with the Khartoum
regime against the Southern rebels. And Russians, it was
clear, had come into the Sudan as military, security and tech-
nological experts. They brought in planes and pilots and
various forms of military assistance.

Materiel from Russia was known to include T-55 heavy
tanks, late model Mig-21 fighter-planes, Mi-8 helicopters,
Antonov 24 bombers, Tu-16 medium bombers, light tanks,
howitzers, artillery and ground rockets. According to African
sources in Washington,[3] Moscow, up to the end of 1970, had
supplied the Sudan with two squadrons of Tu-16 medium
bombers and half-a-dozen AN-24s equipped with rockets, as
well as the late model Mig-21 fighters, helicopters, artilery
and light tanks. One correspondent[4] reported that, according
to a British aircraft mechanic who worked in the Sudan,
Soviet military pilots were ferrying in military supplies from
Egypt in Antonov transports almost daily. At least five of the
largest Antonovs, the An-24s, were reported to have been
converted into bombers. Soviet Mig fighters and tanks were
on show for all to see at a military parade in Khartoum mark-
ing the anniversary of the Nimery military regime.[5]

What was in question was the use to which this *materiel*
was put. In December 1971, Major-General Abdul Gadir, at
that time Chief of Staff of the Sudanese army, in an interview
in Khartoum, gave me a categorical denial of any bombing in
the South. If he meant that there was no bombing at that time,
his claim was to be confirmed a month later by none other
than the opposing general, Joseph Lagu, Commander-in-Chief
of the Southern Sudan Liberation Front, who told me that
the last Russian Mig to drop rockets on their headquarters
in eastern Equatoria had done so in July 1971. Since then, a
few Antonovs had been seen on reconnaisance but there had
been no more bombings.

But, before July 1971, there had been persistent reports of
Soviet helicopters and bombers being used against the rebels.

For example, there was said to have been a raid on the *Anya-Nya* base at Morta (located in a mountainous area on the south Sudanese border with Uganda) in October 1970. According to a Western correspondent,[6] the Sudanese commanding officer told him that, without the Russian-supplied helicopters, the soldiers would never have been able to reach this inaccessible place (which fell to a Sudanese army brigade after a battle lasting twenty-five days in which casualties, mostly civilian, were estimated at 1,000). Other government sources were said to have agreed that without the helicopters their forces would have had little opportunity to attack *Anya-Nya* squads. These squads often operated over such rugged and difficult terrain that it would have been sheer suicide to try to pursue them.[7]

On 25 January 1971 Soviet helicopters supported an attack on the then main rebel base camp at Owing-Ki-Bul ('Hear the Drums') in Equatoria province, which was strafed and bombed. Not only the headquarters but a primitive hospital there (which had turned out 104 trained medicos) was totally destroyed. An eye-witness report said that although most of the able-bodied escaped into the bush, those unable to run for cover died in the air-raid or were killed by two Egyptian commando companies which had arrived within minutes of the air attack. Helicopters, Migs and Antonovs were also said to have made bombing attacks against four other places from the two principal Southern towns of Malakal and Juba. The helicopters were allegedly piloted by Russians.[8]

According to Southern sources,[9] one of the earliest bombing raids was an attack by three Mig jets on the Nuer village of Nyerol in the Upper Nile province, in which cattle camps were bombed on 20 December 1969. The same report gave details of other alleged bombing attacks in which thousands of head of cattle were destroyed; the destruction of a hospital near a place called Magwi on 25 January 1971; and raids on villages in the Palwar region of eastern of Equatoria by Soviet-piloted helicopters and Migs from Juba (capital of Equatoria province).

What evidence is there that Russian airmen took part personally in any of these and other attacks? Much of it would not stand up in a court of law. There was, for example, the testimony by Chief Anderia Gware that soldiers came, some by jet planes and helicopters, and shot people and destroyed crops in April 1971 in his area—the Bari area, fifteen-twenty miles south-east of Juba. Chief Gware reported that, according to his people, the helicopter pilots were white and the people took them to be Russians. On the Ethiopian side of the Sudan border in December 1971 a Nuer refugee told me that in August 1970, at Akobo, on the Sudanese side of the border, he had personally seen four Russian Mig fighters pounding the town by day and night. *Anya-Nya* in the town told him that they had seen Russian pilots getting in and out of the Migs. The Russians were kept at military headquarters —they were not allowed to stay in the military barracks at Akobo and Nasir.

By the middle of 1971 Sudanese pilots were undoubtedly flying helicopters and Migs. On a Sudanese Airways flight back from Juba to Khartoum on 21 December 1971 I met a Sudanese captain named Mohamed Ali who was introduced to me as a helicopter pilot and who told me he had trained in Moscow and had been flying helicopters in the Sudan Air Force for 18 months. He and other Sudanese pilots told me that it took about six months to train an experienced pilot to fly helicopters and that all Sudanese helicopter pilots were trained in Russia. Major-General Gadir confirmed both points to me in Khartoum the next day, and added that it took three years to train a recruit as a helicopter pilot. Diplomatic sources in other countries placed credence on reports from *Anya-Nya* and foreign observers that before the last of the Sudanese pilots were trained to fly such sophisticated machines as helicopters and the latest Mig-21s, at least some Russians (and other East Europeans) flew battle missions for them in the Southern Sudan. It was argued that neither the Russian nor the Sudanese authorities would have wished to entrust these expensive craft to men who had not been fully broken in. One informant told me that the first Sudanese pilot returned from Russia in the middle of 1970 and that Russians had been flying Mi-8 helicopters in 1970 for at least six months and Antonov light bombers from the beginning of 1970. Another informant told me that when the Sudanese pilots returned from Russia, Soviet pilots flew with them in helicopters as co-pilots for at least the first month or so—but he was unable to produce hard evidence of this. According to General Gadir, Soviet instructors were flying in the North but except for this training all pilots flying in the Sudan were Sudanese.

Further pointers to Soviet participation have been dug out. Rudolph Chimelli described in the *Süddeutsche Zeitung* (22 January 1971) how he was a passenger in a helicopter which flew from Juba (capital of Equatoria province) to the town of Meridi, 240 kilometres to the west. The other passengers included Sudanese information officials, other journalists and a couple of government functionaries. The crew consisted of a Sudanese air force officer as captain, Soviet co-pilot in blue overalls (who in fact directed the flight), Soviet navigator, an Egyptian navigator who, except during take-off and landing, occupied the third seat in the cockpit, and two soldiers, armed with heavy automatic rifles, who watched for rebels through open portholes. Wolfgang Hohmeyer, of the Swiss *Sonntagsjournal*, has added to the story. The helicopter was a Soviet-built heavy duty Mi-8 and the Soviet pilot manned the controls at least part of the way. The pilot said to Hohmeyer in German: 'I come from the Urals and I learned my German in Vienna fifteen years ago.' Both Chimelli and Hohmeyer were told that the helicopter was on a routine flight to carry supplies and the officials to Southern towns. But both newsmen were offloaded at one point, to be picked up hours later. Hohmeyer says when he got back on board, the helicopter's floor was strewn with spent machine-gun shells.

With no official statistics available, since neither Khartoum nor Moscow confirmed *any* Soviet presence in the Southern Sudan, estimates published in the western press of Soviet strength there were fairly consistent. According to these reports, between 30 and 60 Russian planes were being used against the *Anya-Nya* by the beginning of 1971. The number of Russians stationed at or near Juba was estimated at between 100 and 200.[10] One report describes them as serving members of the Soviet Red Army and says their principal role was to accompany Sudanese patrols into rebel-held areas and give strategic and tactical advice. The same report talks of a fully equipped training area on an island in Lake No, which is part of the *Sudd*.[11] Another correspondent[12] refers, in March 1971 to a report that a Russian general was commanding troops in Juba. This story has not, however, been confirmed by any other source (to the best of my knowledge), and other observers regarded it as unlikely. But it may be worth noting that ex-Premier Mahgoub told me (in London on 8 February 1972) that after he had made a deal to buy arms from Russia, the Soviet Ambassador in Khartoum came to him early in 1969 and asked if he would amend the agreement (laying down the number of Russian personnel to be allowed into the Sudan) to include a Russian general. 'I said yes and signed the amendment to allow this.'

In December 1970 an American correspondent spoke of Soviet advisers in mufti scattered through the Southern provinces to direct the use of Soviet weapons against the black guerrillas.[13] A number of correspondents who visited Juba (by courtesy of the Khartoum government) reported the presence of Soviet air personnel at the Juba Hotel. Over a period of months the correspondents discovered that the Russians had signed the hotel register as 'Air Force', 'Sudan Air Force' or 'Soviet Air Force'. A Southern Sudanese informant told me that in October 1969 he personally saw two Russian pilots in flying suits at the Juba Hotel and in September 1970 he saw four of them. They were said to be flying food supplies to the town of Torit (about eighty miles south-east of Juba). No-one he knew had seen the Russian pilots in combat. In June 1971 a correspondent writing in a British newspaper[14] said that the five Russians who had shared Juba Hotel with him and had introduced themselves as 'meteorologists' were really Soviet air force men instructing the Sudanese in the use of aircraft and helicopters that had recently been supplied from Russia. Even so, he had noted no evidence of large-scale Soviet involvement in the South. The airfield at Juba was being enlarged with Soviet assistance, but no Russians were actually in charge of any operations. Another correspondent, an American this time,[15] said that one of three Russians staying at Juba Hotel during his visit there was seen to be working on a helicopter at the airport. When General Gadir told me (in December 1971) that there were no Soviet Air Force technicians in the South, I told him that I had personally seen three of them at the table next to me in the Juba Hotel only a few days previously. Gadir said: 'Well, it is possible that they may have come for a special purpose but there are none *stationed* in the South.'

In early July 1970 an American missionary pilot obtained first-hand evidence of the presence of at least two Russian helicopter pilots at Juba. The missionary pilot was flying two women missionary teachers of a Congo government school to a place called Inagura in the Congo (now Zaire) near the Sudanese border, but by mistake landed across the border inside the Sudan. The pilot and his passengers were taken into custody by Sudan army personnel, driven to Juba and then taken to Khartoum. After fifteen days of questioning they were released and flown back to Juba. At the Juba airfield the American pilot saw a Soviet helicopter with two Soviet pilots who were very friendly and showed him the interior of the helicopter. He asked one of the Soviet pilots if he would take them back to his plane near the border. The Russian said: 'I would be glad to, but it could start a Third World War.' When the Sudanese army men saw the American talking to the Russians they whisked him away, and the American missionary pilot and the two girls were escorted by soldiers back to their plane.

Whatever the full facts of Soviet involvement in the Sudanese war may have been, there is no doubt that Southerners in the bush believed that the Russians were actively helping the

Sudanese army to destroy them. It appeared to some outsiders too that for the first time in Soviet history, Russians were fighting and bombing Africans.[16] In a letter to the Pope dated 25 May 1970—the first anniversary of the Nimery takeover—*Anya-Nya* leader, Joseph Lagu (himself a Protestant) stated: 'Even as we write to you, Soviet tanks are rumbling through the streets and Soviet Mig-21 jets are flying overhead in a parade to commemorate African Revolution Day. Yesterday these same tanks and planes were in action in Southern Sudan, killing and maiming our defenceless people, and tomorrow they will return to continue their mission of death and havoc. Our people have grown accustomed to the sight of Russian soldiers directing the Sudanese Arab soldiers in their war...'

In a similarly emotional vein, Lagu addressed an open letter to the Russian leaders. He began by saying that many black Africans had returned from the Soviet Union with vivid descriptions of the persecution of black Africans by the Soviet people. Although he presumed that the mob violence against Africans was not condoned by the authorities, in his view, the general hostile attitude of the people towards black Africans was well summed up in the phrase they used most frequently in describing the Africans—*chorni obezyani*, ie black monkeys. He then went on to draw a parallel between the Soviet role in the recent war in the Yemen and their present involvement in the Sudan. According to Lagu, the Egyptians had been trying between 1962 and 1967 to annex the Yemen to the UAR. Unable to defeat the Yemeni on their own, they called on the Soviet Union to help them. The Soviet government had responded with alacrity, first supplying armaments and then the skilled technicians who were required to replace the inept Egyptians in order to exploit armaments in the manner for which they were designed. The Soviet technicians had performed their jobs proficiently, bombing, strafing and according to the International Red Cross, even resorting to the dispersion of poison gas by aerial bombing when the Yemeni refused to surrender to more conventional bombing attacks.

The Soviet Union, Lagu went on, had also wanted to acquire naval bases in warm water seas, such as the Mediterranean, the Red Sea and the Persian Gulf and intervention in the Yemen must have seemed one way of achieving this objective. Certainly the Soviets must have thought that the acquisition of the Yemeni port of Hudaydah as a Soviet warm water naval base was worth the risk of being censured by world opinion.

During 1970, the letter continued, the Soviet government undertook a new and callous initiative. Just as it had supported Egyptian genocide in the Yemen, the Soviet government came to the rescue of another client state, the Sudan, when it found itself unable to fight its own war of suppression against its nationals in the South. The old iron chain of requirements was again in evidence: first, the supply of armaments in exchange for political and strategic advantages; then the provision of military technicians as advisers; finally, all-in Soviet shoring-up of the military arm of the client state through the use of Soviet troops in direct combat with the adversary of the client state. In return for this direct support, the Soviet government had extracted compensation from the client state in the form of political support and, more tangibly, warm water naval bases—in this instance, Port Sudan and Suakin on the Red Sea—and air bases at Wadi Saidna and Juba. The latter base thrust deep into East Africa, outflanking Ethiopia and Kenya and within easy bombing range of Uganda, Tanzania, Zambia and much of Congo Kinshasa, the site of an earlier Soviet-sponsored revolt against the Congolese government of General Mobutu.

All this, of course, has the ring of blatant propaganda, and it is not too difficult to guess whence the inspiration for it came. The highly charged emotionalism and the use of such terms as 'genocide' do little to contribute to a better understanding of the complexities and involvements of the Sudanese conflict. I have reproduced the letter's contents in some detail, however, because in spite of the extravagant language, the letter did give the burden of the Southern Sudan's case against the Soviet Union as seen through *Anya-Nya* eyes.

The *Anya-Nya* claimed they had evidence for their allegations that Soviet machines and military technicians were used in destructive attacks against the South. In another open letter[17]—on this occasion to President Kenneth Kaunda of Zambia—General Lagu said that he and his people had seen Russians moving about in the streets of Juba where they were based, flying the Mi-8 helicopters and firing rockets and guns at them from these helicopters. They had heard the screams of wounded Russian pilots and had buried the bodies of Russian airmen who had perished with their helicopters.

Whether the *Anya-Nya* tribesmen can distinguish the screams of wounded Russians from other men's screams is one thing. But General Lagu showed correspondents the corrugated door of a Soviet-built helicopter claimed to have been shot down over Morta—and the *Anya-Nya* published a photograph of Lagu holding the door. One British source[18] told of grisly dental evidence that a few Russians had been killed in attacks on *Anya-Nya* camps. According to his report, the *Anya-Nya*, knowing that the identity would be challenged, had cut off the dead men's heads and had had the dentistry established as Russian by dental experts. General Lagu told me that between September and November 1970, during raids on his camp at Morta, two Russian helicopters were shot down and two dead men in them were identified as Russians. They had Russian features and *Anya-Nya* medical staff confirmed that their dental bridgework was Russian.

Support for at least some of the allegations of Soviet involvement in the Sudan came also from quite different kinds of sources. In January 1971, an African academic working at an American university[19] took two American correspondents[20] to task for saying that the Sudanese strife was 'a bloody Soviet-backed civil war'. History, the professor said, had showed that the Sudanese war was a direct result of nineteenth-century European imperialist partitioning policies in Africa in general and the British Cape-to-Cairo grand design in particular. Nonetheless, he found their exposure of the growing Soviet arsenal of weapons in the Sudan 'commendable'. In his view, the Soviets' politico-military ambitions from the Mediterranean Sea to the Indian Ocean were very obvious and as dangerous to the Africans as Euro–American military establishments in and around Africa.

Sometimes, too, a denial can be significant. In an article entitled 'Soviet Union is not supporting Genocide in Southern Sudan',[21] the Sudan Afro–Asian Solidarity Committee vigorously denied claims that the Russians had taken over the air base of Wadi Saidna, near Khartoum, and that Soviet pilots, based there, had flown Tupolev 16 and Antonov 24 bombers in attacks on the South. 'These claims,' said the article, 'are completely untrue. There are no Soviet military personnel in the Sudan—there are only civilians assisting in the peaceful development of North and South Sudan.' The committee admitted that there were Soviet pilots at Wadi Saidna but described them as commercial air transport pilots flying freight as part of the Soviet assistance programme. And Wadi Saidna, it added, was not a Soviet air base but the base for long-range penetration attacks against Israel by the Sudanese and UAR forces.

The real sting in General Lagu's open letter to the Kremlin leaders came, of course, in his reference to Moscow's desire for naval bases at Port Sudan and Suakin and air bases at Wadi Saidna and Juba. (How this may be seen to fit into the wider Soviet strategy will be examined in the next chapter.) Few reports in the western press on the Sudan caused such a stir in Moscow and Khartoum as the allegation in *Time* magazine (1 March 1971) that the Russians had begun to construct a naval base at Port Sudan. Denials were put out simultaneously in Khartoum, Moscow and Cairo. To show how ignorant the authors of the *Time* piece were, Mr Mohamed Al Amin Abdalla, a Sudanese diplomat then in Moscow, rapped them over the knuckles for talking about six million black Southerners in the Sudan when records showed there were fewer than three million.[22] The point at issue, however, was really whether or not a Russian naval base was being built at Port

H

Sudan. Technically speaking, the denial was justified—there was no naval base being built *at* Port Sudan—although the contention that ships calling at Port Sudan from all parts of the world could testify to the fact was not all that convincing. Port Sudan was not exactly a keypoint for world shipping in 1971. The real question was whether or not the Russians were building or helping to build a naval base in the Port Sudan *area*.

Reports began to filter through which lent weight to the allegations. Apparently Port Sudan itself was developed as a civilian port with the aid of Yugoslav and Egyptian technicians and Egyptian finance.[23] The Russians were reported to be building a small to medium size naval base ten miles away from the civilian port. A member of the Sudanese mission to Moscow of February 1970 confirmed that one of the conditions laid down by the Russians and accepted by General Nimery for Soviet aid to the Sudan was that the Russians could build a naval base in the Port Sudan area. According to a former Sudanese government source, the naval base was situated between Port Sudan and Suakin. (Since Suakin is twenty miles from Port Sudan, this squares with reports of the naval base being ten miles from Port Sudan.) All the reports[24] agreed with the original report that the Russians were installing Sam-2 anti-aircraft missiles to defend the base.

What were the reasons behind the undoubted Soviet interest in the Sudan? And how were Soviet interests to be affected by the crisis in Soviet–Sudan relations which followed the abortive July 1971 coup in the Sudan? I shall discuss these two questions in the next chapter.

Notes to this chapter are on page 183

CHAPTER NINE

What Did Moscow Want?

Basically, Soviet involvement in the Sudan fitted into the larger Russian strategy of increasing Soviet power and influence in the Middle East and East Africa, hunting for bases in the Indian Ocean and trying to outflank the Chinese. But there were other factors which could make for tactical shifts.

In mid-1971, Mr Boris Ponomarev, Secretary-General of the Communist Party of the Soviet Union, on a visit to Cairo, told Mr Muhammad Heykal, editor of *Al Ahram*, that the Soviet scale of foreign policy priorities put the Middle East as third after Vietnam and Cuba.[1] This could have been intended as a helpful comment on the facts of life; but it looked more like a warning to the Egyptians to watch their teeth if they wanted the Russian hand to go on feeding them. The Russians began to make Egypt one of their main bases at a time when the main object of Soviet policy was to establish a naval presence in the Mediterranean. Up to 1970 Moscow's main interest was in the Mediterranean followed by the Indian Ocean and the Red Sea (in that order). But once its presence in the Mediterranean had been firmly established, Soviet strategy turned to the more distant Indian Ocean—and so Soviet interests moved south from the Suez Canal area. In this pattern of thinking the Sudan could have a significance for the Russians comparable with that of Egypt. It has been suggested[2] that in the event of peace between Egypt and Israel and the subsequent re-opening of the Suez Canal, the Soviet Union would no longer need to bother much about its communications with the Indian Ocean through Suez. The Sudan, on the other

hand, could provide it with valuable bases on the Red Sea—
which, strategically, is part of the Indian Ocean—and could
act as a valuable supplement to the facilities already established at Aden and Socotra farther south. In the sphere of
oceanic strategy, the Sudan was therefore no less important
than Egypt. Indeed, the argument went, the Russians might
find that in the Sudan they had a base which was, in the long
run, of more use to them than Egypt.

In some ways the Soviets could be seen to be following the
old British imperial designs—in an age of faster communications and developed technology. So long as the Middle East
remained in a state of tension, their pivot in the Arab world
was still Egypt—key to the passage through the strategically
important Suez Canal and Red Sea. Russia had to hold the
Sudan because the Nile passes through the Sudan and who-
ever holds the Nile holds Egypt by the throat. (The Russians
no doubt had studied the story of how, when Arab nationalism
grew in Egypt, Britain, as controlling power, used the Sudan
threat. 'If you don't behave,' Britain told Egypt, 'we can take
the waters away from you.' The British threatened to irrigate
the Sudan with consequent loss of water to Egypt—the Allenby
Ultimatum.[3])

In its strategic plans for the 1970s, Moscow had two lines of
thought: (1) the British Victorian concept (the Russians could
still be considered 'Victorians' themselves in terms of imperialist ambitions) of Egypt as key to the Arab world; (2) the
need for a secure lifeline with the strategic Mediterranean as
a large backdrop. Looking forward to the day when they would
be able to manoeuvre between the Mediterranean and the
Indian Ocean, the Russians built up a permanent navy going
up and down the Mediterranean all the time. In the Indian
Ocean, and particularly the western part, the Russian fleet
was relatively small. But the build-up of Russian mercantile
and fishing fleets was described as 'tremendous'—a 'show-the-
flag' tactic which had paid off elsewhere and has become part
of the new Russian tradition. Following its historic quest for
warm-water ports, the Russian presence was becoming in-

creasingly apparent across the breadth of the Indian Ocean. The patient build-up of the Soviet fleet in the service of Moscow's global policy was announced in advance by the Soviet naval Commander-in-Chief, Admiral Sergei Gorshkov, when he said on 28 July 1968 that the Soviet navy had now been converted into an offensive type of long-range armed force which could exert a decisive influence on the course of an armed struggle in 'theatres of military operations of vast extent'. This navy was also able to support state interests at sea in peace-time, he added.

If, in addition to its two cruiser-sized helicopter carriers, the Russian navy decided to build attack carriers, the whole strategic picture could change. But so long as they lacked carriers—and in spite of having an estimated force of ninety nuclear-powered submarines—the Russians needed land and air bases, as well as naval bases, in order to guarantee future plans in the western part of the Indian Ocean. Their plans for bases included:

Hudaydah, in North Yemen. This looked doubtful for the Russians because of the North Yemeni government policy.
Aden. Russian-aided harbour deepening was said to be in progress and Soviet harbour pilots to be operating here.[4] An Adeni journalist also reported in the Lebanese newspaper, *Al-Hayat*, on 15 June 1969, that the National Liberation Front government of South Yemen had 'pawned' the port to the Soviet Union and had given the Russians fishing monopoly rights.
Berbera, in Somalia. This naval base was built north of the old port in 1970–1, at a cost of several million pounds to the Russians, for medium-sized warships—but the Somalis had no vessels larger than patrol boats and a promised frigate or destroyer, so it seemed obvious for whose use the base was intended.
Mersa Matruh, in Egypt. This was reportedly planned, before Sadat sent the Russians packing, as a major naval base for the Russians.

Hargeisa, Somaliland. The Somali air force is small, but significantly this airbase was built to accommodate Mig-21s. Hargeisa is near Berbera and it was thought apparent that the Russians were interested in it as air cover for the naval base.

Alula (west of Socotra, on the south-west side of the tip of the Horn) where African diplomatic sources said a new naval base was being built.

Russian warships were reported to rendezvous frequently at the island of Socotra; the Russians secured port facilities at Mauritius in July 1970 in a three-year agreement; a little later shore facilities for Soviet vessels were reportedly negotiated on this same island which is 1,200 miles east of the South African coast.[5] To that list was added Port Sudan, Wadi Saidna (reported to have been handed over by the Russians to the Egyptians) and Juba, in the Sudan. But later, the Russians were left with no bases in the Sudan and little hope of gaining any.

The extent of Soviet investment in the Sudan remained a close secret. A conservative estimate put the total Sudanese accumulation of Russian military supplies at the time of the 19 July 1971 coup in excess of £30 million—many times the value of economic 'aid' from that source. In January 1972, ex-Premier Mohamed Mahgoub told me that President Nimery had received at least £70 million of army equipment from Russia; and I was informed in the same month by an African diplomat that Soviet equipment for the Sudan was running at about £35 million a year and that, thanks to Soviet aid, the Sudanese military budget increased from an estimated £37 million in 1969–70 to an estimated £65 million in 1970–1.

In return the Russians were able to have a substantial key presence in the Sudan. Mr Mahgoub told me that his own agreement with Moscow had specified the number of Russians permitted to come into the Sudan.[6] President Nimery, in an interview[7] in August 1971, said that the maximum number of Russian military and civilian technicians in the Sudan had been 250 (a number considerably lower than some estimates reported in the previous chapter). Sudan was able to claim that it had to pay dearly for Russian help. In return for weapons, tractors, and consumer goods and three million dollars in cash, the Soviet Union in 1970 got 300,000 bales of Sudanese cotton;[8] and about 60 per cent of the cotton crop was pledged to the East Bloc in 1971.[9]

The dispute between Moscow and Khartoum which came in the wake of the abortive Communist coup was a turning point in Soviet–Sudanese relations. But even before the July crisis some disillusionment in the Sudan with the Russians had already set in. So you could find a Sudanese businessman complaining privately that the Russians were greatly over-pricing their tractors, which were not nearly as efficient as the western-manufactured ones which formerly came into the Sudan. After the July squabble, criticisms were voiced openly. Mr Idris Mahmoud, Sudanese Minister of Economy, for example, is reported to have disclosed that the Russians had been charging prices for goods sold to the Sudan in exchange for cotton that were 30 per cent above world market levels. At the same time the Russians resold the cotton at 10 per cent discount, thus undercutting the Sudan in its traditional world markets. 'In any given year of trading with Russia, we have been losing between £25 million and £30 million for every £100 million of trade,' the Minister reportedly said.[10]

One Sudanese minister is quoted as saying that the Russians had violated international practice by foisting goods on the Sudanese at 30 to 35 per cent above world market prices.[11] The Sudanese were also said to have been blaming the Russians for the fact that industrial growth in the first part of the five-year plan—drawn up by the Russians—had fallen as much as 50 per cent below expectations. For their part, the Russians, with a fine sense of irony, were blaming the Sudan-ese socialist regime for having rushed into nationalisation without adequate preparations. Meanwhile Sudanese experts were reviewing all contracts under Russia's five-year plan and summarily cancelling the questionable ones.[12]

The details of the Moscow–Khartoum dispute were well
publicised. The Russians (and the Bulgarians) were involved
in the short-lived Communist takeover from the Nimery
government. Leading Sudanese Communists in the coup were
executed after Soviet pleas for clemency had been ignored.
The Soviet, and its allied and satellite, press mounted an
angry campaign against the Khartoum government. With a
show of no less indignation Khartoum said this was an internal
matter and gave an ultimatum to Moscow to stop its campaign
of interference. Khartoum withdrew its ambassador to
Moscow.

But the cross-interests were complex. Both sides blew hot
and cold—perhaps neither could have done otherwise. It soon
became evident that Nimery was ready to forgive the Russians
for their role in the coup. He was seen to have made the same
kind of gesture to Messrs Brezhnev and Kosygin as the late
President Nasser made in the 1950s to Mr Krushchev over
Egypt's stand against Communism. In a study paper which I
wrote for the Institute for the Study of Conflict (London)[13]
I noted that, although President Nimery could not ignore
Moscow's challenge to his authority, a final break with the
USSR seemed unlikely at that time. The Sudanese were
dependent on Moscow for spare parts for the arms they needed
to continue the war against the Southern rebels—with no
signs of peace yet in the offing. For the Sudan, dependence on
Moscow seemed a necessary embarrassment. (A few months
later, President Sadat, in neighbouring Egypt, appeared to see
no discrepancy between a high-level purge of Communists in
Cairo and a visit to his patrons in Moscow.) And the Russians
had no desire to be cold-shouldered out of the Sudan.

When the news of the July 1971 coup broke, the first
impression was that it was in line with the blueprint for
Communist takeovers in Africa set out in the Soviet textbook,
The Political Parties of Africa, published by a team of Soviet
Africanists a few months previously.[14] The Russians must have
reckoned at first that the coup-leaders had a chance of holding
on to power. Why, otherwise, did the Soviet Ambassador to

Khartoum, Anatoly Nikolayev, go out on a limb by being the only foreign envoy to call on coup-leader Hashim al-Ata in the Sudanese capital? (According to a United Press International report, 26 July, the plotters were seen saluting Soviet officials.) It was a major miscalculation by Moscow—and much was to flow from it.[15] But as soon as it was seen that the coup had misfired, another old Moscow tradition was followed: the Kremlin steadfastly refused to take on itself any share of blame for a blunder committed by Moscow hard-line Sudanese Communists. The Russians, however, saved their own faces and showed their good faith to the International Communist fraternity by condemning the executioners of the Sudanese Communist leaders. As soon as the Communists were cold in their graves, the propaganda campaign was quietly dropped.

Then Moscow set about mending its broken fences with the reinstated Nimery. One example of Soviet thinking in the context of Russia's relations with the Third World Communists is provided by Professor R. A. Ul'yanovski[16] who wrote, in September 1971, that the anti-Communist measures which had been carried out in a number of countries were unquestionably making it difficult to achieve any national understanding between Marxist–Leninists and National Democrats —in fact, between progressive forces generally. Even when these measures had only been temporary, they had affected both the substance of national democracy and the course of the National Liberation Movement. 'However, proletarian parties do not yield to emotion but proceed with objective clear analysis'—a broad hint. Another Russian writer,[17] noting that the major revolutionary democratic regimes were starting to repress Communists and other progressive forces, asked whether one should therefore conclude that the policy of co-operation with revolutionary democracy was unjustified.

But the doublethink is an essential part of Soviet policy, the rigidities of which are no less than its flexibilities. It is clear that despite the setbacks the Russians have suffered in the decade in which most of the African states became independent (examples of which are the expulsion of the Soviet missions in Guinea and the ex-Belgian Congo), they are still sticking to a long-term plan which is to set the entire continent on to the path to Soviet-style Communism. What is more, they appear to believe that progress to that end has been, and is being, made.

It was all very well for Muhammad Heykal, editor of *Al Ahram*, to remind the Sudan in August 1971—in respect of the Soviet Union—to distinguish between differences between friends and contradictions between enemies.[18] How was Moscow to convince President Nimery that its espousal of an activity in which the head of a friendly state was deposed by force and imprisoned, and officers faithful to him slaughtered, could even remotely be classified as friendship? President Nimery clearly remained unconvinced. He might have been prepared to forget as well as forgive. But it became evident that if the Soviets were capable, not for the first time, of treating a Third World Communist Party as expendable, they were also capable, if the need arose, of taking up its case again. Nearly eight months after the coup, President Nimery, in an interview, told a correspondent[19] that, even though the coup had failed, the Soviet Union was still harbouring runaway Sudanese Communists. This accusation was symptomatic of the suspicions which Moscow had succeeded in implanting in the President's mind. This was the real damage Moscow had done to its position in the Sudan. This was the broken fence that remained unmended.

With the first signs of a Russo–Sudanese estrangement in July 1971, the Chinese tried to step into the breach[20] by promising to make up any reduction of trade and aid from the Soviet Union and to double their own trade with the Sudan (estimated at £12 million a year in both directions). The Chinese offered a £14 million interest-free loan to the Sudan government, on top of a loan of £15 million negotiated the previous year. The Sudan also received some Chinese weapons (resistance forces in the South claimed to have captured army rifles described as Chinese-manufactured copies of Russian originals). But (although some Sinotologists see a Chinese

Red under every bed in Africa) too much should not be made of this. The Sudan was still far from being a Chinese sphere of influence. And the loans were not quite as generous as they sounded. The Chinese spread their loans in Africa over ten years and do not give money but projects, which include Chinese labour. A Khartoum to Port Sudan highway and a water scheme in western Sudan were among the projects.

Of far greater significance were the signs of a Sudanese *rapprochement* with the West. After nationalisation moves had brought industries to a critical state, General Nimery slowly and quietly began to revise the policy in favour of at least a partial return to the private sector. This brought prospects of a renewal of foreign investment; negotiations got under way with Western Germany, the United States, Britain and Kuwait, among other countries, as well as with the World Bank. The opening of peace negotiations with the Southern rebels brought a new attitude of sympathy for Khartoum from many countries.

Encouraged by these trends, President Nimery, on 2 March 1972, gave the clearest indication to date of his intention to try to reduce Soviet influence in the Sudan. In newspaper interviews published simultaneously in Beirut[21] and Abu Dhabi[22], he was quoted as saying that if the Soviets refused to supply Sudan with the spare parts it needed, it would abandon Soviet armaments and buy from some other country. He had no illusions that it would be an easy matter to get the Russians off his back. In December 1971 a highly placed observer in Khartoum (who did not wish his identity disclosed) told me that there were still Russians in key posts in many fields of activity. But the Sudanese are clearly determined to be independent of the Soviet Union or any other foreign power.

Notes to this chapter are on page 184

CHAPTER TEN

Opposing Elements

The 1969 May revolution, apart from inheriting what appeared to be Africa's most intractable civil war, inevitably made enemies. Some of them might in time be neutralised or even won over in part or in whole. But even when, in February and March 1972, the Sudan was seen to have taken a major step towards ending its biggest problem, the war with the South, President Nimery was well aware of the continued existence of discordant and disruptive elements—not least of all in his own North. In an address at a rally at Omdurman (discussed in the introduction to this book) in March 1972, the President pointed a finger at 'troublemakers'. In an obvious, although unstated, reference to the late Joseph Garang (Minister of State for Southern Affairs) and Garang's personal hard-line Communist cohorts, Mr Nimery said that the treachery of those entrusted with the implementation of the policy in the South, as well as that of their 'comrades' in the North, had slowed down the progress of the regional autonomy plan. These people had used their official positions to further selfish, partisan interests.

In an equally obvious reference to hard-liners on the Right as well as the Left, the President told the mass meeting that there would be people who would try to trap the government into breaking the cease-fire so that the Addis Ababa agreement became nothing more than mere ink on paper. There would also be trouble from those people who had lost power after the revolution and who were jealous of the new government's success.

The main opposing elements were the Communist Party on the Left, and the *Ansar*, conservative, religious Muslim Mahdist 'followers' (the word *Ansar* means followers) on the Right. Old rivals of the *Ansar* were the traditionally pro-Egyptian *Khatmiyya* religious group dominated by the Mirghani family, its hereditary leaders. The *Ansar* ran the Islamic-dominated UMMA ('Nation') party and the *Khatmiyya* wielded influence over the National Unionist Party (NUP) and later the People's Democratic Party (PDP) followed by the Unionist Democratic Party (UDP). Both sides had come together in coalitions before political parties were dissolved in the Sudan and the distinction between them became blurred. But leading figures in and behind the banned parties continued to present potential dangers to the Nimery government. On the extreme Right, were the disruptive, implacably anti-Communist, Muslim Brotherhood (fanatical Islamic traditionalists). There were dissidents in the civil service, the universities, the trade unions and the army. There was the openly hostile but untested United Sudanese African Liberation Front under the Reverend Phillip Ghaboush Abbas. And there were personalities around whom anti-government moves could develop—the most notable being Sharif Yusuf al Hindi and Sadiq el-Mahdi. Much of the opposition was later to be soon over or withered away. Some of it remained.

Generally acknowledged to have been the largest and best organised Communist Party of any country in Africa or the Middle East, the Sudanese Communist Party, before its mauling in August 1971, was estimated to number between 30,000 and 50,000 card-carrying members—with the Khartoum government putting the figure at 10,000. The Communist Movement was introduced into the Sudan at the end of World War II by Sudanese students and teachers returning from Cairo. By the end of 1950 the party had gained a large measure of control over trade unions and formed a number of front organisations, including the Students' Congress. Its leadership came from middle-class, urban, rather than proletarian, origins, and the rank and file came from the middle and working classes in the towns. What really built up the party was its brilliantly organised underground resistance to the Abboud military regime—party membership expanding from about 750 in 1958 to an estimated 3,000 to 10,000 in 1965 (all statistics are difficult to check in the Sudan, not least Communist Party memberships). The Communists began to wield an influence out of all proportion to their numbers. The Soviet Union was the chief source of funds for the Sudan Communist Party since its inception—an acknowledgement of the fact that the bulk of the membership was oriented towards the USSR, although fewer than twenty per cent were believed to be avowedly Marxist and activist. There was a small pro-Chinese group within the party which called itself the Revolutionary Leadership Faction, but this faction played an insignificant role in the drama that was to engulf the party and the country.

Although the Communist Party was banned along with other political parties in the Revolutionary Command Council's clean sweep after its accession to power in May 1969, General Nimery offered the Communists a deal—the sharing of power in return for their support for a new socialist programme for the country. By a narrow majority the party's twenty-five-member Central Committee rejected the offer. The party then split into two sections, each with its own leadership and apparatus. The 'hard-line' party which stayed outside the government was headed by the Secretary-General, Abdul Khaliq Mahgoub, an internationally-known Marxist leader of high intellectual calibre who was regarded as the brain of the Sudanese Communist Party and said by some to be the most important Communist in the Arab world.[1] The so-called 'soft-line' section was headed by Mawja Ibrahim (a less impressive personality than Abdul Khaliq Mahgoub) and Ahmed Suleiman. A deal with the apparently acquiescent section was made. The pro-Marxist Babikir Awadalla was appointed the regime's first Prime Minister ,and a number of known Communists were taken into the government. Mr

Ibraham became Minister for Labour and Mr Suleiman first ambassador to Moscow and then Minister of Industry. Another Communist, Mr Farouq Abu Isa, became Minister for Foreign Affairs. But the split in the party had been over tactics and did not run deep. Mr Joseph Garang, Minister of State for Southern Affairs (although he was able to keep his job until he was executed after the July coup) turned out to be a hard-liner in soft-liner's clothing. In April 1970, Abdul Khaliq Mahgoub was exiled to Cairo.

In November 1970 General Nimery, who had been finding out more and more unpalatable facts about his Communist support, struck again. This time he dismissed *three* of the Communists' main supporters in the Revolutionary Council of Ministers, Colonel Babakir el-Nur Osman, Major Hashim al-Atta, and Minister of Interior, Major Farouk Hama-dallah (who, if not a party member, was the next best thing). There were so many other changes that it was difficult for an observer to keep up with who was doing what and where. There was less confusion about the 'why' of these shifts. By February 1971 a disillusioned Nimery was announcing that his regime would 'crush and destroy' the Communist Party. A few months later he was to tell Southerners—during his campaigning for the plebiscite which was to vote him in by an overwhelming majority as President—that the Communists were 'people whom we trusted and they stabbed us in the back'.

It was now open war between the Nimery government and the Communists. And on 19 July 1971 the Communists put the Sudan on to the front pages of the world's newspapers. Led by Major el-Atta, rebel troops seized and deposed President Nimery in Khartoum. In London Lieut-Colonel Babakir el-Nur Osman was installed as leader of the new government. Within seventy-two hours it was all over and Nimery was back in power. Playing the part of prosecutor, Nimery questioned Babakir (who had been taken off a BOAC plane while flying home to Khartoum and handed over to the President). Babakir denied prior knowledge of the plot against

Nimery. Then why had Babakir been named leader of the new rebel government, Nimery asked.

Within a few days not only the coup-leaders, including Babakir el-Nur Osman and Major Atta, but other Communist leaders had been hanged: Garang; Abdul Khaliq Mahgoub (who had returned from Cairo, enjoyed a few months of freedom, been arrested and escaped from jail); Shafie Ahmed Shaikh, secretary-general of the Sudan's federation of trade unions and a Lenin Peace Prize winner. The speed and ruthlessness of the executions shocked the world. But President Nimery told correspondents that it was the conspirators who had been ruthless when they murdered Nimery's officers during their brief taste of power—and that he had indisputable evidence that the convicted Communist leaders had been directly responsible for the overthrow of his government.

At least 1,000 and probably double that number[2] of people were netted in mass arrests of known and suspected Communists. There were further summary trials, although of a less spectacular nature than the drama of the leaders who had been taken out to die in the hot sun. The great majority of the rank and file were later released, but it was clear that the Sudanese Communist Party had lost a great deal of ground. That it was discredited, at least for the time being, was no less evident. In the South few tears were shed for Joseph Garang—even if Grass Curtain[3] (official mouthpiece of the Liberation Movement) found it incumbent on itself to pay a tribute to the man with whom it had clashed so fiercely and so often in the past. (The propaganda motivation behind this encomium to a dead opponent and the shock at his swift dispatch was all too blatant—this was not one of Grass Curtain's finer moments.) The Southerners scarcely needed President Nimery to tell them that a Communist minister had actually delayed regional autonomy for the war-torn South.[4] Southern leaders had long been convinced that Mr Garang put party interests before Southern interests.

But then Communism had generally failed to make the kind of impact on Southern intellectuals it had made on

Northern ones. None of the Southern leaders I have personally met, inside or outside the Southern Liberation Movement, subscribed to the Marxist solution. Mr Garang and his associates did make a few converts in the South, but, according to Southern intellectuals with whom I have had discussions, they were not the people from whom leadership and direction were likely to come. If the July coup had succeeded (or if the Communists ever managed to regain a measure of control in the running of the State) would the South have accepted and worked with the Communists? Almost anything is possible in politics, but prospects of a substantial and enduring Southern acceptance of Communist solutions in almost any circumstances remained very doubtful. In his first statement in London as leader of the short-lived take-over regime, Lieut-Colonel Babakir el-Nur Osman had promised to implement regional autonomy and encourage democratic institutions in the South,[5] and his close associate, Major Farouk Hamadallah, former Sudanese Minister of the Interior (dismissed by General Nimery in November 1970, and also to die at the executioner's hands) is reported to have said that regional autonomy depended on popular participation in the South, which the new regime would enlist.[6] But it is worth noting that even in the immediate excitement of the apparent downfall of the Nimery government, these assurances were received with scepticism by Southern representatives.

The Sudanese Communist Party undoutedly suffered in the purge which followed; but whether the Party was permanently crippled, let alone destroyed, was another matter. In the euphoria of victory plucked from defeat, the Nimery government talked of having smashed the Communist Party. But there was reason to believe even then that Communism and the Communists—with an unknown amount of secret support, or promise of future support from Eastern Europe, was far from dead. Certainly it would be no easy matter to replace cadres of the level of a Mahgoub, a Shaikh or a Garang. But in an attempt to show that they were not a spent force, Sudanese Communists, at an undisclosed venue, a few days

J

after the abortive coup, elected a new Party Secretary to succeed the executed Mahgoub—Ibrahim Nogood, a prominent party member for years and one of the thirty Sudanese Communist leaders who were still on Khartoum's wanted list.

Nimery's government reacted no less sternly to pressures from the Right. The Aba island affair gave rise to much controversy. It is generally believed, although never officially admitted by *Ansar* sources, that the *Ansar* religious leader the Imam el-Mahdi, had led what has been described as a 'rebellion' against the government.[7] *Ansar* civilians reportedly tried to kill General Nimery with spears and clubs when he visited the town of Kosti, near the *Ansar* stronghold. In retaliation for this attempted assassination, General Nimery's forces attacked the *Ansar* island of Aba, on the White Nile with the support of about twenty-five Mig combat aircraft. Up to 3,000 *Ansar* civilians were allegedly killed and many arrested while others fled to Ethiopia. The Imam was killed while trying to escape. Government sources in Khartoum told me the death toll was less than 1,000; and they denied that there had been any bombing—let alone that the bombing went on for five days.[8] Ex-Premier Mohamed Mahgoub, himself a member of the *Ansar,* gave me a very different account. According to him, many thousands of people were killed on the island by bombs and rockets from Migs, 'which were definitely flown by Egyptian pilots as there were no Sudanese pilots capable of flying a Mig accurately at the time'. According to the *Ansar,* Aba was a 'massacre'. Mr Mahgoub denied that the attacks had been provoked by an attempt on President Nimery's life. 'It is not the *Ansar* way to assassinate people,' he said. 'Nimery's real object was to try to crush all political opposition. But the *Ansar* are as strong as ever. If the British were not able to crush the *Ansar* in all their years of rule, Nimery couldn't do it in one attack. The Aba issue will never be forgotten. There were representatives of every *Ansar* tribe on the island. Nimery, therefore, made enemies of all the *Ansar*.'[9]

Whatever the rights and wrongs of the Aba island episode,

the *Ansar*, although weakened, remained a force to be reckoned with. *Ansar* members and their families were estimated at one time to number between three million and four million persons. Although not nearly as tightly organised as the Communist Party, they continued to possess the machinery for political organisation. After the death of the Imam el-Hadi el-Mahdi, the only visible leader of the *Ansar* was his nephew, Sadiq el-Mahdi (who was exiled to Cairo four days after the onslaught but was reported, the following year, to be under virtual house arrest in Port Sudan. Sadiq and his uncle had been rivals for power over the UMMA party which the *Ansar* traditionally controlled. Sadiq, then aged only thirty and regarded as a 'progressive' (a relative term), won a victory over the traditionalist Imam when Sadiq succeeded Mohamed Mahgoub as Prime Minister in June 1966. Less than a year later El-Hadi el-Mahdi gained the upper hand and Sadiq, defeated in a vote of confidence on 15 May 1967, was replaced by Mr Mahgoub. UMMA split into a pro-Sadiq faction (UMMA–Sadiq) and a pro-Imam faction (UMMA–Imam), while Mahgoub continued as Prime Minister, heading a coalition in 1968 which included UMMA–Imam. But when Mahgoub was overthrown in 1969 by Nimery, the Imam and his nephew healed the split to oppose the new regime.

The UMMA party (of which Mr Mohamed Mahgoub remained a veteran, but inactive, leader in exile) was traditionally anti-Egyptian, but was capable of strange alliances. So at one time you could find anti-Egyptian *Ansar*–UMMA and pro-Egyptian *Khatmiyya* NUP in harness[10] and, later in the day, when Nimery had banned all political parties, a flirtation between the conservative, religious *Ansar* and the anti-religious Communists—and this in spite of Communist support for the Nimery government's attempt in March 1970 to put down the rebellion led by the Imam.[11] Mr Mohamed Mahgoub told me[12] that during his period of office before the Nimery takeover he had excellent relations with the Communists 'who gave no trouble at all' and that he had for years been friends with Abdul Khaliq Mahgoub, whose execution

he described as a great tragedy for the Sudan. In the opinion
of some observers, the *Ansar* secular nationalists lack the militancy found in other groups. There was a paradox. The one
thing that has always interested the *Ansar* leadership is power.
They did seem to retain the capability of taking over organisation in the event of an uprising—from almost any direction—
against the Nimery government. But when out of power, the
Ansar tend to be flexible in their tactics; and their very flexibility made *rapprochement,* endurable or not, with the
Socialist government a possibility. In Sudanese politics (which
continue to thrive in the absence of official political parties)
it is traditional for feelers to go out in all kinds of directions,
plausible and otherwise. It was well within that tradition
that the Nimery government, having confiscated the busi-
nesses and lands belonging to both the dead Imam's family
and the rival Mirghani family (which head the *Khatmiyya*
sect) should be reported as trying to win the political allegi-
ance of the followers of these groups by convincing them that
they would get more benefits if the state owned these enter-
prises.[13]

Although the *Khatmiyya* sect was estimated to have been
almost as large as the *Ansar* (both are Islamic brotherhoods),
it was not nearly as cohesive or politically effective because
its membership was widely dispersed among diverse (Muslim)
tribes and urban groups. Originally supporting the National
Unionist Party, the *Khatmiyya* in 1956 formed a new party,
the People's Democratic Party (PDP), which after the civilian
takeover of government (from General Abboud's military
regime) in 1964 was allied with a series of leftist organisations
and was reported to receive military aid from China. Towards
the end of 1967 the NUP and the PDP merged to form the
Unionist Democratic Party. The *Khatmiyya* continued to be
heavily subsidised by Egypt. The Mirghani rulers of the
Khatmiyya maintained some influence behind the scenes in
Khartoum. But the *Khatmiyya* seemed unlikely to pose a
serious threat to the ruling government without the blessings
of their Egyptian patron.

Generally recognised as the most militant of the minority groups in the North, the Muslim Brothers are mostly highly educated, modern Arabs whose aim is to turn the Sudan into a militant, purified Islamic state. The ultra-conservative Muslim Brotherhood (Al-Ikhwan al-Musilmun) movement originated in Egypt and the Sudanese "Brothers" continued to have strong sympathies with the suppressed Muslim Brothers in Egypt. They were, therefore, opposed to the Cairo government and, lacking strong backing, tended to support UMMA against *Khatmiyya*. Well-organised, both as a religious and a political force, they have always been fanatically opposed to the Communists. It is their fanaticism which makes them a never forgotten factor in Sudanese history.

An unknown quantity was the 'United Sudanese African Liberation Front' (USALF) headed by Phillip Ghaboush Abbas, a former Anglican churchman, and claiming to represent more than four million non-Arabised Negroid peoples of western, central and eastern Sudan (all part of 'Northern' Sudan). A member of Nyimang tribe of the Huba people of central (Northern) Sudan and born in the Nuba Mountains area of Kordofan province, he became leader of the General Union of Nubas (GUN) in 1964 and was elected a Member of Parliament in 1965. Five separate Negro organisations with both civilian and military cells were brought together in April 1969 under Abbas's leadership to form the USALF. In a book, *Black Power in the Sudan*, he describes how his movement organised a coup against the Mahgoub government on 29 May 1969. But General (then Colonel) Nimery beat him to it on 25 May and the Abbas coup attempt fizzled out. Abbas writes: 'Two days after Nimery's coup we had a chance to kill him.' But, he continued, there had seemed to be little point in doing so. If he had been killed, another like him would have taken his place. Besides, the USALF members were not keen on cold-blooded murder. Another coup—this time against the Nimery regime—planned by Abbas for 18 July 1969, did not get started, and Phillip Abbas fled the Sudan on 16 July a few hours before troops came to arrest him.

His book makes a number of interesting statements. In February 1968 he tables a motion of no confidence and mounts enough votes to topple the Mahgoub government—which is able to stay only because the President (Ismail el Azhari) finds an excuse to dissolve the Assembly. In Addis Ababa, in 1969, Abbas meets the Emperor of Ethiopia, Haile Selassie, who, according to Abbas, tells him frankly that although he sympathises with the Liberation Front, he can offer it no material help. Abbas and his fellow USALF members are free to leave Ethiopia to present their case elsewhere, but he himself feels bound by the OAU Charter.

In Jerusalem USALF representatives are shown the kind of weapons that Israel might be prepared to give them. They are ancient rifles from World War II and even earlier, which would be of little use against the modern arms that the Sudan government was now receiving from the Soviet Union. It appears to Abbas and his colleagues that the Israelis are perhaps not really serious in their offer of support, and that they will have to look elsewhere. At Fort Lamy he asks President Francois Tombalbaye to allow them to establish a base on Chad territory near to Darfur. The President demands to know what he can expect in return and Abbas explains how they think they could help him. The President says he will consider the problem and call them later. 'We are still waiting,' Abbas says woefully, adding that he is becoming increasingly convinced that no one outside Sudan is interested in the plight of the black people of that country or thinks that they can do anything to free themselves from the Arabs.

Abbas claims that in October 1970 the USALF concluded a formal agreement with the group led by Sharif Yusuf al-Hindi in which they agreed to work together militarily. Sharif al-Hindi, former Minister of Finance and Economy in the Mahgoub coalition government, was regarded as perhaps the most formidable Northerner in opposition to the Nimery regime. He inaugurated a group called the Sudanese People's Resistance Front in exile in December 1969. He was not a man to be discounted.

Abbas also tried to form a Black Power military coalition with the *Anya-Nya*. But, he says candidly in his book, Lagu refused to meet him, saying that he could not trust him now that he was working with the Arabs. Abbas claims that there was some military co-operation between Northern Negro groups and the *Anya-Nya* in the Upper Nile. If this was so, it was obviously on a very limited scale. Mr Abbas told me[14] that about eleven Negroes from Darfur and Nuba were fighting along with the *Anya-Nya*. The reason there were so few was that it was difficult to get weapons and difficult to get to the South. *Anya-Nya* spokesmen had told me (before peace negotiations with Khartoum opened in Addis Ababa) that they would take Abbas and his organisation seriously only when the USALF was able to stage some kind of real revolt in the North. Mr Abbas's answer was that guerrilla warfare was not practicable in the North—no cover was available in Southern Kordofan and Darfur, while the Nuba Mountains were not suitable for hit-and-run tactics.

Abbas, in exile and nominally sentenced to death *in absentia*, continued to dream his dream of a Black Power take-over in a federal Sudan (of eighteen provinces and eight federal units) controlled by its non-Arab majority. He continued to claim a power base in the non-Arab areas in the North and potential support inside the army (with its crack Negroid troops). If both the Northern and the Southern leadership was less than impressed, they might have been underestimating both the man and his possibilities. And only time would tell how Khartoum's new relationship with the South would affect the Negroid parts of the North. The USALF was not consulted in the Addis peace negotiations.

But only time, too, would tell whether the Nimery regime would prevail against pressures that might build up against it, severally or jointly, from such disparate (but not inevitably incompatible) sources as the *Ansar* (with or without the support of the Communists), the Muslim Brothers, Sadiq el-Mahdi, the Mirghanis, army dissidents and other plotters. Would an improved economy and an improved security as a result of the ending of the war in the South bring the Sudan the stable government it so badly needed after a record of seven changes of government since independence in 1956?

After Addis, the Nimery government looked more secure and stable than any government the Sudan had in the past. In discussions with the author at the beginning of 1972, General Joseph Lagu and certain other Southern spokesmen made no secret of the fact that they would rather have dealings with General Nimery than with any other Northern leader, Sharif al-Hindi included. After Addis, Lagu was to become one of Nimery's leading supporters.

Notes to this chapter are on page 186

CHAPTER ELEVEN

The Sudan's Neighbours

The claim that the Sudanese is a bridge between the Arab world and Africa took on a new significance and credibility when the war between the largely Arab North and the African South stopped. While the war raged the Sudan was regarded by outsiders as more of a battleground between the two worlds. Even in the heat of the moment (and there were some tense moments) no African country ever seriously considered becoming militarily involved in the conflict. The Egyptians, however, were undoubtedly involved on the government side, although the extent of their involvement was disputed. By the end of 1970, Egypt was estimated to have between 5,000 and 10,000 troops in the Sudan, as well as a large number of advisers and technical experts, with an Egyptian army college functioning in Khartoum. Reports of Egyptian air and ground support for the government in Southern Sudan were even more insistent than similar reports about Soviet participation in the war—and were no less vigorously denied. There were reports of Egyptian air personnel being seen at the Juba Hotel and Egyptian pilots taking part in offensive sweeps on *Anya-Nya* areas, as well as taking part in the attack on the *Ansar* island of Aba in March 1970—which Khartoum denied. Two Egyptian commandos were reported to have taken part in the attack on the rebel stronghold of Owing-ki-Bul on 25 January 1971. One report spoke of 100 Egyptian Migs at the Wadi Saidna airport north of Khartoum—outside the range of Israel's jets.[1] There were conflicting reports on whether or not the Egyptians (and the Libyans) actively helped General Nimery to stage his successful counter-coup against the Communist takeover in July 1971. ('We fight our own battles ourselves," Major-General Gadir, then Chief of Staff of the Sudanese Army, told me in Khartoum five months later.) But a cabinet minister in Libya disclosed that both Egypt and Libya had *prepared* to intervene militarily if the counter-coup failed.[2]

But relations between Egypt and the Sudan have never actually been as good as they have sometimes been made to appear. Since the overthrow of King Farouk—who thought the Sudan belonged to him—the Egyptians adopted an official posture of respect for Sudanese independence and paid lip-service to the principle of unity without strings between the two countries. The Mirghani family (see Chapter 10) always supported the idea of the closest possible ties with Cairo. But other elements in the Sudan continued to fear and distrust Egypt and to be suspicious of 'bonds without bondage' where their powerful neighbour up the road was concerned. When, in 1972, the Nimery government began to receive economic assistance from the United States and Western Germany, while maintaining the coolness, developed in the July 1971 coup, with the Soviet Union, the Egyptians grew openly impatient with President Nimery. Egypt, it should be remembered, was still at that time the Soviet Union's client state. The first hint of an open deterioration between Cairo and Khartoum came in an accusation by Lebanon's proEgyptian mouthpiece, the daily *Al Moharrer,* that Khartoum had moved away from the Federation of Arab Republics and preferred to co-operate with 'reactionary' African regimes and the Western powers instead.[3] Much play was also made of the fact that President Nimery had 'purged his government of Nasserites'.

How true were these allegations? As President Nimery reorganised his government after the new deal with the South, the influence of pro-Egyptians was cut down along with pro-Marxist influence. The Sudan continued, however, to behave with propriety towards Egypt and to maintain the best pos-

sible relations with the rest of the Arab world. But Libya's
Qadaffi unhappy at the influence of non-Arab Southerners in
the new, post-war Sudan, began to show an ambivalent attitude toward the Nimery regime and to encourage its
opponents. And the prospect of the Sudan's joining the Arab
Federation became less favourable for a number of reasons.
When President Sadat announced (on 17 April 1971) the
agreement joining Egypt, Libya and Syria in a common union
with 'one President, one flag, one anthem and one federal
capital', he explained that the Sudan, which, he said, was
linked to the three countries in a co-operative alliance, would
not join the Federation at the time because of special circumstances.[4] Two days later President Nimery was reported to
have talked of the Sudan's 'ultimately' joining the Federation.
A dispatch from Khartoum by Egypt's Middle East News
Agency quoted Nimery as saying that the Sudan must prepare
a new constitution and build a strong political organisation
as a prerequisite. But in December 1971 Mr Oman El Hag
Mousa, Sudanese Minister of Information, clarified the issue
when he told me that the Sudan would not enter the Arab
Federation without the consensus of all its people.

Northern friends later gave me what they felt to be strong
reasons both for and against joining the Federation. The 'pro'
school considered that it was necessary in terms of Sudan's
loyalty to the Arab cause and that the mutual benefits would
be considerable. Those against said variously that Sudanese
entry into the Federation would be unwise because of (1) the
economic disparity with Libya; (2) fear of being dominated
by Egypt; (3) the damage it would do to Khartoum's new relationship with the South. Southern friends were adamant
that Sudan's entry into an Arab Federation would impede
unification of the country. By 1973 it had become evident to
almost everyone in the Sudan that the Sudan had no intention
then of sacrificing its independence to become part of any new
state. For Khartoum entry into an Arab federation seemed
to have become a dead issue. But a common currency, postal
and customs union was still on the cards.

Whatever the final outcome on the form of unity, the Khartoum government appeared to have no uncertainties about the spirit of Arab unity. As part of its commitment to the Arab cause, it maintained a firm, but not obtrusive, anti-Israel posture. There were insistent allegations of Israeli 'interference' in the Sudanese conflict and of Israeli participation in a conspiracy to overthrow the Sudanese regime. Reports of Israeli military aid for the *Anya-Nya*—denied by Israeli and *Anya-Nya* official sources—came from Khartoum, Cairo, Moscow and also from a number of Western commentators. Israeli officers, helped by West German mercenaries, veterans of Biafra, were reported to be training and supplying the rebels with equipment ranging from American medical kits to Russian and Chinese weapons captured from the Egyptians and the Palestinians.[5] A Sudanese diplomat claimed that Israel was using rebel bases on the Uganda front for the training of European and African mercenaries, who were then sent into the Sudan.[6] There were frequent reports—unconfirmed—of Israelis parachuting arms and supplies from an unmarked DC3 to the rebels' Owing-ki-Bul camp.[7] The supplies were said to include heavy machine guns, bazookas, hand grenades, ·303 World War II rifles and old land mines of Russian and British origin, 'all captured by the Israelis from the Egyptians during the Six Day War'.[8] Sudanese secret police claimed that General Lagu was not only in close personal touch with Israel (which was never very strenuously denied) but sent other *Anya-Nya* warriors there for military training.[9] In the trial which opened in Khartoum on 1 August 1971 against Rolf Steiner, a West German mercenary accused of directing guerrilla operations in the Southern Sudan,[10] an alleged statement by Steiner was read alleging among other things that Israel had bases in Southern Sudan, Ethiopia and six miles from the Sudan border in Uganda. It was also alleged at the trial that a military training school had been established in South Sudan through the assistance of Israel and that the Israelis had taken part in the laying of mines in rivers. The point was made elsewhere, however, that whatever assistance the rebels re-

ceived from Israel (or any other outside source) it was insignificant compared with the volume of Soviet military aid
which poured into Northern Sudan. If Khartoum was far more
bitter about Israeli aid for the rebels than about alleged interference from a variety of other sources, the Sudanese quarrel
with Israel tended to recede when Sudan's own civil war
receded. It later flared up again.

The Secretary-General of the Organisation of African
Unity, Diallo Telli, came to Khartoum to add his voice to the
condemnation of foreign mercenaries at the Steiner trial. But
the Sudan government's solid relations with the OAU were in
no way dependent on the continued presence in that key post
of Mr Telli (whose leadership was considered in some quarters
to be of doubtful value). The OAU—in spite of a number of
appeals from Southerners to intercede in the Sudanese conflict
in the interest of human rights and 'the existence of African
unity'.[11]—maintained a strictly neutral attitude on the North–
South conflict, holding it to be an internal matter. When
peace negotiations started in earnest, early in 1972, the Organisation, however, played a meaningful part. The Emperor of
Ethiopia guaranteed the security of the Southerners in his
own name and that of the forty-one-nation OAU;[12] and the
announcement that an agreement had been concluded in
Addis Ababa was made by Mohammed Sahnoun, an Assistant
Secretary of the OAU, who had been attending the negotiations in an advisory capacity.[13] Freed from the strains of civil
war, the Sudan could hope to play an important role in the
Organisation.

A year previously Faruq Abu 'Isa, then Sudanese Foreign
Minister and leader of the Sudanese delegation to the OAU
ministerial meeting in Addis Ababa (27 February 1971), made
it clear that the Sudan still adhered to its firm stand of non-
interference in the internal affairs of other states, especially in
those of fraternal African countries. Indeed, it was his view
that the Sudan had constantly worked to develop better
relations between fellow Arab states and to promote the joint
interests of all the nations of the African continent. On the

other hand, his country was determined not to allow anyone to interfere in its internal affairs. His government would not be goaded into abandoning the principles to which it was so fully committed.[14]

There were good reasons, from Khartoum's point of view, why it was considered necessary to combine its assurances of good faith and good intentions towards African neighbours with a warning—and no less reason why, from their point of view, some of these African neighbours regarded the assurances with some scepticism. For one thing, there were different basic attitudes on Israel (which had a close relationship with Ethiopia and Uganda at a time when Khartoum was blaming Tel Aviv as the chief author of its guerrilla troubles). While Ethiopia's scarcely-concealed sympathy with the rebel Southern Sudanese seemed like an affront to Khartoum, Addis Ababa charged that the Sudan government supported and gave refuge to Eritrean Liberation Front (Arab) rebels against Emperor Haile Selassie's rule.

The Khartoum–Kampala situation was, if anything, more contentious. Mr Faruq Abu 'Isa went on (in his speech at the OAU ministerial meeting) to spell out the trouble. General Amin, he said, had again been talking about the Sudan. This time he had not accused it of interference but of something far more serious. According to Omdurman Radio,[15] the Minister then went on to read the statement in which General Amin had compared what was going on in the Southern Sudan with what was happening in South Africa, and in which he had expressed his attitude on the British supply of weapons to South Africa. This statement, said the Minister, was blatant interference in Sudan's internal affairs.

From Uganda came accusations of Sudanese aid for the deposed Ugandan President Milton Obote, then a refugee in the Sudan. And in the most serious incident to date, a Uganda military spokesman announced, on 15 December 1971, that fierce fighting had been taking place just inside Uganda between Sudanese government troops and Southern Sudanese guerrillas. He said that unless the Sudanese forces withdrew by the following morning Uganda would use maximum force to protect its citizens and preserve its territorial integrity.

The following day, however, General Amin announced that the Sudanese troops had been withdrawn, the situation was back to normal and he was inviting a Sudanese delegation to Uganda to talk things over. On 26 January 1972, in Kampala, President Amin received the Sudanese Minister and Adviser to the Ministry of Southern Affairs, Peter Gatkwoth (a Southerner), who led Sudan's delegation to the first anniversary celebrations of the Second Republic of Uganda. The President told Mr Gatkwoth that Uganda wanted peace and good relations with the Sudan because they could only develop their countries when there was peace. President Amin assured the Sudanese delegate that the refugees in Uganda had been warned not to indulge in any subversive activities against their various countries.[16] As a further assurance of good neighbourliness, General Amin offered Uganda as a venue for proposed peace talks between President Nimery and General Lagu—a gesture that was much appreciated in Khartoum although in the event the negotiations were ratified in Addis Ababa.[17] And what seemed at the time to be the last remaining cloud over Sudan–Uganda relations disappeared when, in April 1972, Uganda severed all ties with Israel by expelling all 700 Israeli advisers and diplomats.

Sudan's relations with Ethiopia had been pursuing a similar course (except that for a while the Emperor maintained friendship with Israel). Negotiations for reconciliation opened with a visit to the Sudan of an Ethiopian delegation, from 21 to 24 March 1971. In talks at Foreign Minister level, both sides agreed to develop trade relations, form a land, sea and river transport committee, improve communications, review the 1960 cultural agreement and take preparatory steps towards a settlement of the boundary question between the two countries. At the beginning of November 1971, President Nimery paid a six-day state visit to Addis—and the Emperor reciprocated with a state visit to the Sudan for the Independence anniversary celebrations in January 1972. A cultural agreement, providing for the exchange of scholars, cultural delegations and materials for use in information media, was signed; and it was agreed to convene the joint boundary commission early in the year. The question of re-defining the borders had long been a difficult one, but it was evident that a new era in relations between the two countries had opened. Khartoum quietly put a stop to Eritrean rebel activity in the Sudan and Ethiopia could no longer be regarded as a haven for elements hostile to Khartoum. To set the seal on the new friendship, the Emperor, more than anyone else, was personally responsible for the successful outcome of the North–South peace negotiations.

With the cessation of hostilities in the Southern Sudan, the tensions caused by the presence of large numbers of Southern Sudanese refugees in the neighbouring countries began to ease. According to figures prepared for the United Nations High Commission for Refugees in September 1970, there were 176,000 Southern Sudanese refugees in the neighbouring states, including 59,000 in the Congo, 20,000 in Ethiopia, 72,000 in Uganda and 25,000 in the Central African Republic. Various other sources found these figures conservative, estimating the number of refugees overseas at a probable 250,000 or more.[18] There were repeated allegations from Khartoum that guerrillas were going in and out of these countries masquerading as refugees. In order to reduce the danger of provocation, both the Central African Republic and the Congo (Zaire) pulled the refugee camps away from the border. When the settlement to end the war was signed, neighbouring governments as well as organisations concerned with the humanitarian needs of these refugees, heaved a sigh of relief.

As Mr Omar El Hag Mousa, Minister of Information, said to me in Khartoum (on 22 December 1971, when peace negotiations were still in doubt), with what I felt was a quite moving candour: 'All African governments are fed up with the Sudan. They will all be pleased to see the problem finished.'

Notes to this chapter are on page 186

CHAPTER TWELVE

One Sudan or Two?

Almost from the moment a Southern political movement was born in the Sudan in the early 1950s, it pressed for federation. In October 1954, the first Liberal Party conference—at Juba —passed a resolution demanding federal status for the South. With independence in 1956 the campaign continued; but in 1958 Mr Mohamed Ahmed Mahgoub declared in Parliament that the governmental Constitution Committee had given the Southern claim for federation very serious consideration and found that it could not work. In spite of this rebuff—only one of many—the pressure for federation continued until it was smothered by the 1958 military takeover. Again in 1965, at the Round Table Conference, the case for federation was put. Again nothing happened. Southerners were to say—with justification—that the North did not keep any promise to give real consideration to the South's desire for federation. Northerners were to say—also not without justification—that it was never quite clear what was meant by 'federation' in the Sudanese context.

SANU and the Southern Front came up with two proposals at the Round Table Conference. One was for a plebiscite in which the people of the Southern Sudan would have three possible choices: (1) federation; (2) unity with the North; (3) separation (to become an independent state).[1] A later and final proposal provided for the creation of Northern and Southern regions, which amounted to two separate states joined together by common services.[2] Once more nothing came of either proposal.

K

Southern politicians at no stage formally abandoned the principle of federation. But in the years ahead many of them privately agreed that if the South gained some form of autonomy in a unified Sudan, some degree of flexibility would be required from both halves of the country. Military spokesmen in the *Anya-Nya* after the breakdown of the 1965 conference began to talk more and more in terms of a separate, liberated Southern Sudan. Therefore, by the time that the Nimery regime began to make its first offers of regional autonomy for the South, Southern opinion itself was already divided between (1) some form of Southern independence within one Sudan; and (2) secession—and possibly the union of the Southern Sudan with an East African country. For a long time the case for secession was taken quite seriously.

Those favouring the South's integration with the North maintained that Southern Sudan was not viable on its own. In answer to the separatists' suggestion that Southern Sudan might be better off in a federation with an East African country such as Kenya, they pointed out that no East African country had shown the slightest interest in such a proposition. Besides which, they argued, the North would never agree to split the Sudan, and without the North's approval, a separate Southern state would have no security. Separatist talks of breaking away from the North by force was, in the long term, unrealistic.

The Nimery government's new Southern policy of regional autonomy was at first regarded by leading Southerners with much suspicion because of broken promises in the past and also because they felt that Joseph Garang, the Southerner put in charge of the programme, was not a man they could trust. But it soon became evident that the Nimery regime was going a long way to give Southerners positions of trust in the South; and some, although not all, of these Southerners were men held in some respect by their compatriots. In this situation the 'one-Sudan' school of thought started to gain ascendancy over those favouring secession and a fight to the bitter end.[3]

The war had been too long and too bitter for a quick and

easy shift from the battlefield to the conference table. But on 7 March 1971 reports began to appear of secret diplomatic exchanges in London between representatives of General Nimery's government and of General Lagu's rebel *Anya-Nya* forces.[4] A month later Mansour Khalid, newly appointed Sudanese Ambassador to the United Nations, told a UN press conference that Sudan had entered negotiations with a genuine revolutionary movement in its rebellious Southern provinces. He said that a group of honest people in the South had misgivings about the government's offer of autonomy and wanted to negotiate more guarantees.[5] One of the many delaying factors was the absence of any direct channels of communication between President Nimery in Khartoum and Lagu, an elusive figure in the Southern Sudan bush. From his headquarters at Owing-ki-bul, Lagu wrote, on 11 August 1971, that the Southern Sudanese Liberation Movement was as anxious as it had always been for a negotiated settlement and he called on General Nimery to meet the movement's representatives to determine conditions which might bring a final end to the war and atrocities in South Sudan.[6]

The World Council of Churches (whose headquarters are in Geneva) played a part in making a dialogue between the two sides possible. In April–May 1971 Abel Alier was the leader of a government delegation[7] which visited Scandinavia to explain the Sudan government's policy in terms of President Nimery's Declaration of 9 June 1969 granting regional autonomy to the South. The government attached importance to the visit because there was a strong pro-Southern lobby in all the Scandinavian countries—with the Southern Sudan Committee of Norway being particularly active—and the Southern case had a wider and better presentation in Scandinavia than anywhere else. During the visit Mr Alier met representatives of the World Council of Churches (WCC) and invited them to visit the Sudan. This invitation was accepted. I learned from other sources in Scandinavia during a visit in October 1971 that some members of the WCC delegation to Khartoum thought that the Sudan government's offers of jobs and training to Southerners were politically motivated and therefore regarded with suspicion by Southern leaders. In spite of this they believed that everything should be done to try and open channels of communication to the South. According to Vice-President Alier, the WCC followed up its visit to the Sudan by offering to mediate between the Sudan government and the rebels. In October, the WCC told the Sudanese government that the rebels were ready to meet the government's fundamental condition which was that any talks between government and rebels should be on the basis of a united Sudan.[8] In other words, the rebels were ready to talk.

At the beginning of November 1971 new groundwork was laid for peace negotiations during General Nimery's state visit to Ethiopia. The Emperor of Ethiopia had taken the initiative to end the Sudanese war. President Nimery was accompanied by Abel Alier (Garang's successor as Minister for Southern Affairs) who was the principal figure on the government side in the peace moves. When President Nimery left Addis Ababa, secret talks continued between a delegation headed by Alier (and containing Southerners in the government administration and Arabs) on the one side and a group of Southern representatives of the *Anya-Nya* on the other. I was in Addis myself at the time and I learned that, although the discussions were inconclusive—at times even sticky—they did pave the way for the successful negotiations in February 1972.

Up till the November talks in 1971 the *Anya-Nya* had demanded the following pre-conditions to official negotiations:

(1) a cease-fire, with government forces confined to barracks;
(2) political recognition for the SSLF (Southern Sudan Liberation Front) as the negotiating equal of the Sudan government;
(3) an international forum for the Southern case, with 'summit' discussions in a neutral African country under a neutral African chairman, with international observers present.

The SSLF had also expressed the view that Southern Sudan should hold a referendum to make the final decision on a proposed agreement.[9] This proposal was quietly dropped. Other concessions were made on both sides before the full-scale negotiations. The *Anya-Nya* did not insist on a cease-fire before the negotiations. They broadened their representation to include the politician Ezbon Mondiri.[10] They did not press for a neutral chairman. The government, which had earlier insisted that talks be held inside the Sudan, agreed to hold them outside.

The negotiations of February 1972 turned out to be far more fruitful than either side had dared to hope. At the end of December 1971, the *Anya-Nya* leadership had drawn up revised recommendations for a new constitution for the Republic of the Sudan. As a compromise between secession and regional autonomy the constitutional draft proposed: [11]

(1) a federation consisting of the two existing Northern and Southern regions, with a federal government in Khartoum under the President, and a separate regional government in each of the two regions;

(2) national defence, external affairs, currency and coinage, communications, nationality and immigration, foreign trade, customs and excise and higher education to be federal responsibilities;

(3) the judicial systems—federal and regional. Certain legislation, however, to be subject to ratification by both the regions, each of which would have a Prime Minister.

There still seemed a wide gap between what the Southerners demanded and what the government was likely to agree to. Anticipating the Southern demand for two regional governments, I asked Hilary Logali, Commissioner for Equatoria (in a discussion at Juba on 17 December 1971) what he thought of the idea of regional autonomy for the North as well as the South. Although himself a Southerner, Logali thought there was virtually no chance that the North would agree to a two-region autonomy proposal. Altogether it seemed in December 1971 that the negotiations being planned for February 1972 in Addis would still be preliminary ones and that hard bargaining lay ahead.

When I met Mr Omar El Hag Mousa, Minister of Information, in Khartoum on 23 December 1971, he made an offer on behalf of the Sudan government to meet the *Anya-Nya* and other Southern dissidents for official negotiations either inside or outside the Sudan and said the government would welcome help from any neighbouring country to bring about peace. 'If you have a chance of making contact with General Lagu,' he said to me, 'please give him a message from General Nimery that the President is willing to meet him personally at any place at any time. If Lagu wishes, his old commander in the Southern Command of the Army, General Bagher, whom he trusts, can also meet him.' When I asked the Minister if he intended to make this offer to Lagu known through official channels, he replied: 'No. There are no direct channels of communication. We sometimes communicate through the British Broadcasting Corporation but on this occasion we would like to do it through you.' I had gone to Khartoum as Chief Foreign Correspondent of Forum World Features, an international features agency syndicating articles and reports to newspapers in more than fifty countries; and I was therefore able to get wide coverage for the offer—and General Lagu's subsequent acceptance in principle.

My meeting with Lagu took place 'somewhere in East Africa' in January 1972.[12] The *Anya-Nya* guerrilla leader said it was not very encouraging that Khartoum's December peace offensive had coincided with a new military offensive (which had taken the army to the Uganda border). He agreed, however, that it was possible that Khartoum's motivation was to come to the peace table with as much military advantage as it could get; and he described General Nimery as the most reasonable leader Khartoum had had. He asked me to tell Khartoum that he would be glad to meet President Nimery, or General Bagher, or Mr El Hag Mousa, or any other Arab

Sudanese leader or leaders. He said it would be most conven-
ient for him personally if such a meeting could be held in
Uganda (although he would not rule out other neighbouring
countries) and he wondered whether President Amin would
repeat his offer of Uganda as a venue. I put this question to
the Ugandans in Kampala a few days later. President Amin's
reply, repeating his offer (which he made on two previous
occasions) was given to me by the President's Press Secretary,
Benny Kanangyeyo. President Amin said he would be happy
to mediate if both sides wished him to do so.

In the event the negotiations in Addis Ababa turned out to
be conclusive, and a meeting in Kampala proved unnecessary.
The negotiations began in mid-February 1972. The leaders of
the government delegation included Vice-President Abel
Alier, Dr Mansour Khalid, Minister for Foreign Affairs, and
Major-General El Bagher, Minister of the Interior. The
Southern delegates were Ezbon Mondiri (chief of delegation),
Mading de Garang (spokesman), Dr Lawrence Wol Wol,
Angelo Voga, Oliver Albino, Fredrick Maggott, the Rev Paul
Puet and Job Adier.[13] Both sides feared that the negotiations
might break down on the issue of security; and according to at
least one report,[14] Emperor Haile Selassie found it necessary
at one point to call the negotiators to his palace and guarantee
the Southerners security against reprisals.

The talks ended on 27 February with a joint announcement
by the Khartoum government and the South Sudan Liberation
Front that agreement had been reached. The agreement formally ending the war was signed in Addis one month later
(27 March) by General Lagu on behalf of the South and Dr
Mansour Khalid, now Sudanese Foreign Minister, on behalf
of the government.

The agreement, as outlined by President Nimery,[15] em-
bodied a draft organic law to organise regional autonomy in
the Southern provinces; amnesty; the transitional period;
cease-fire; armed forces; return and resettlement of refugees.

The organic law—the Southern Provinces Regional Self-
Government Act, 1972—came into force on 3 March 1972.

Under the law the provinces of Bahr el Ghazal, Equatoria and Upper Nile constituted a self-governing region to be known as the Southern Region. It established a People's Regional Assembly as the legislative body for the Southern Region, and a High Executive Council. It defined the following as national matters not subject to the legislative and executive jurisdiction of the Southern Region's Executive Council or Regional Assembly: national defence; external affairs; currency and coinage; air and inter-regional river transport; communications and telecommunications; customs and foreign trade (except for border and certain commodities which the regional government might specify with the approval of the central government); nationality and immigration (emigration); planning for economic and social development; educational planning; public audit.

The People's Regional Assembly was given the power to legislate for the preservation of public order, internal security, administration and the development of the Southern Region in cultural, economic and social fields and in particular with regard to: regional financial resources; machinery for regional and local administration; traditional law and customs; prisons; state schools; local languages and cultures; town and village planning and construction of roads; trade, local industries and markets and traders' licences; public hospitals; health services; animal health; tourism; zoological gardens, museums and exhibitions; mining and quarrying; police and prison recruitment; land use; pest control; forest products and pastures; self-help schemes.

The law guaranteed freedom of movement, citizenship rights, personal liberty, equal opportunity of education, employment, commerce and profession, freedom of religion and conscience, protection of labour and freedom for the minority to use their language and develop their culture. The basic agreement provided that Arabic would remain the official language of the country, but that English should be used as a working language in the Southern region, as well as any other local language that might prove useful for efficient administration or under certain practical circumstances. The new Amnesty Act reaffirmed amnesty to all who took part in the mutiny and worked actively against the government. Special commissions were to be established for the repatriation of refugees with the co-operation of the UN High Commission for Refugees and host countries. Juba became the capital of the Southern Region and the seat of the regional executive and legislative body.

The following appointments were made to the Executive Council: Abel Alier, President; Hilary Logali; Toby Maduot; Luigi Adwok; Joseph Oduho; Ezbon Mondiri; Mading de Garang; Nyasio Goma; Michael Wal; Elia Lupe; Samuel Aru. General Lagu was given a general's post in the army in Khartoum. Lawrence Wol Wol became a minister in Khartoum. There were many other important jobs to be filled and a number of Southerners to fill them.

For the South the March 1972 accord opened a new chapter of opportunities and a new chapter of problems. There was the enormous problem—in practical, economic as well as human terms—of the resettlement of hundreds of thousands of refugees and other displaced persons. Indeed, one of the major tasks facing the leaders of the new Sudan was that of winning sympathy and practical aid from other countries in order to be able to fund short-term and long-term programmes for this rehabilitation.

There were also internal problems which no outside force could do much to help to solve. One of these was the composition of the army in the South. The President announced (in his 3 March speech) that this question would be dealt with by a military technical committee. Elements of the *Anya-Nya* rebel force were to be phased into the army, and it was easy to see where frictions were likely to arise. But then the whole question of the future of the *Anya-Nya* was fraught with difficulties. Certainly there was a cease-fire—and for the good reason that the moment the agreement was announced without waiting for the official date of the cease-fire, the army simply ceased firing. But it was one thing for the educated leadership of the *Anya-Nya* to accept peace terms and make immediate efforts to honour them in the letter and the spirit. It was another thing to expect thousands of men—representing a host of different tribes who had come together and sunk some of their differences for the sole purpose of fighting an enemy they believed to be their oppressors—suddenly to understand and accept the fact that the 'enemy' was no longer an enemy but a 'partner'. Major-General Fadlella Hammad, the new Sudanese commander in the South, took a realistic view when, after accompanying President Nimery on a ten-day tour of the South, he reportedly made the comment that it would take four or five months before all of the *Anya-Nya* had learnt of the cease-fire. And, in his view, there would be some *Anya-Nya* who would never stop fighting.[16] In the event, the early success of *Anya-Nya* integration seemed almost too good to be true.

It became all too clear that Gordon Muortat Mayen was not speaking for himself alone when he denounced the agreement as a fraud;[17] and he must certainly have added to the confusion in the minds of people in the bush and some of those in exile when he alleged that the majority of the *Anya-Nya* movement's field commanders and senior officers had told his so-called African National Front that they had not been informed of the Addis peace talks and opposed the points already accepted by their so-called representatives there.[18] Whether or not some of the leaders objected, it was doubtless an exaggeration to say that they were in the majority.

There is a gap in the records on what exactly took place between the signing of the draft agreement on 27 February 1972 and the ratification on 27 March 1972. The intention, as set out in the draft agreement, was that it would be ratified by President Nimery and General Lagu in person (or through their authorised representatives) in Addis on 12 March. It is known that the fifteen days' delay was due to doubts expressed by Lagu and some of his colleagues on some of the terms. The South Sudan Liberation Movement then prepared an amended draft which it was hoped Mr Alier would ratify on behalf of President Nimery on 27 March.

Under the proposed amendments the Southern Region would have had a Prime Minister instead of a President of the High Executive Council and he would have been elected by the Regional Assembly and not appointed by the President of the Republic. Certain powers now vested in the President and the central government would have been vested in the Regional Premier and a Regional Council of Ministers. There would have been two official languages—Arabic and English —instead of one: Arabic (with English the principal language for practical purposes). Significant differences were demanded in the composition of the army in the South, with assurances written in to make it an all-Southern army by the end of a five-year period.[19] There was some confusion about the amendment and its timing, and it was not ratified. Instead the 27 February agreement was issued by President Nimery as a national law. Personal assurances were, however, given that the feelings of Southerners as reflected in the proposed amendment would be taken into consideration and not ignored. And when it came to the point, on 27 March, General Lagu signed the document ratifying the original 27 February agreement.

An argument developed in the South on whether the *Anya-Nya* commander had done the right thing or the wrong thing in accepting a *fait accompli*. Some went so far as to accuse him of unconditional surrender. Others felt it was an act of statesmanship and took the line that it was the spirit of the agreement and not the letter which would count in the long run.

I must repeat the points I made in the introduction to this book: the mutual antagonisms, mistrusts and suspicions between North and South, with their widely different cultures, date back to long before the start of the Sixteen Years' War. It was too much to expect that they could be removed by a stroke of the pen. Each side had to make concessions beyond what had previously been regarded as desirable or even acceptable. Inevitably there were interests inside and outside the country which saw, or chose to see, the agreement as a surrender, a sell-out or an act of weakness. And there were some who said—whether justifiably or not—that some of their leaders had been rather quick to accept positions in the new government, and that in particular the rebel supremo, General Lagu, would have served his followers better if he had remained behind to help them to iron out their difficulties instead of going so early to his new government army post. But these criticisms were soon overshadowed as the basic economic issue of developing the country came to the fore.

To an observer closely interested in the Sudan and the Sudanese people, but striving to be as objective as possible, there still seemed—on the morning after the agreement—as much reason for hope as for fears. The agreement was basically realistic: it did not attempt an identity of incompatibilities but sought to recognise and entrench the separate interests of North and South on the one hand and their common interests (economic and political) on the other. The question for the future was how well this balancing act could be made to work. It would not serve the cause of peace in the Sudan to minimise the possibility of new obstacles and setbacks.[20]

There were, however, encouraging signs. Apart from the many commendable efforts on the home front, new initiatives were apparent in the Sudan's foreign policy. As a result of a visit to Pope Paul VI by Foreign Minister Khalid, in November 1971, the Vatican announced (on 29 April 1972) that it had reached agreement with the Sudan to establish full diplomatic relations; and there were reports that the first trickle of returning foreign missionaries to the South had begun. The South needed all the help it could get from the outside world in the form of money or skilled workers from the developed countries. Educators, planners, technical advisers, even the missionaries had a part to play in the South again.

Notes to this chapter are on page 187

Not Angry but Hungry

I returned to the Sudan in November 1972, eight months after the peace agreement, and again in March 1973. I was impressed beyond all expectations by the progress evident in terms of human relationships between former enemies.

I found that the integration of the *Anya-Nya* into the army had gone far more smoothly in the first year than I had dared to hope. Six thousand *Anya-Nya* were being integrated with 6,000 Northerners to form the army in the South. Other *Anya-Nya* were being integrated into the police and prisons departments. I spoke to them at all levels. All seemed happy.

At Torit, where the war started, I spoke to two joint commanders, an Arab Northerner and an African Southerner, and I was struck by their easy cameraderie. Lieutenant-Colonel Saturnino Ariha, former Commander of the 1st Battalion of the 1st Brigade of the *Anya-Nya*, and Colonel Kamal Beheir, Acting Officer Commanding Torit District, had fought on opposite sides although on different fronts. They were now on such obviously good terms that they swopped war stories. It was almost like captains of opposing teams fraternising after a football match.

At the Juba barracks I met Captain Isiah Paul, an *Anya-Nya* who fought the Northerners for nine years and had now been chosen to head a hand-picked unit of 123 *Anya-Nyas* to act as a bodyguard for President Nimery in the Republican Palace Guard. 'Nimery knows he can trust the *Anya-Nya*,' a Southerner told me.

Wherever I went in the South, whomever I talked with,

157

President Nimery's personal popularity was unmistakable. Southerners spoke to me freely, criticising many things and many people—particularly some of their own leaders. But almost everyone had a word of praise for Nimery. 'He is our hero,' General Joseph Lagu told me. 'Whatever else may be wrong,' a former refugee back from Uganda told me, 'Nimery at least has brought us peace.'

Over lunch in the Khartoum University Club, Mohamed Omer Beshir tried to explain to me how former enemies could apparently become reconciled so quickly. 'You have to understand,' he said, 'that we are all Sudanese. Basically this is more important than being Northern or Southern, Arab or non-Arab.' Peter Nyot, a Southerner, who was chairman of one of the People's Assembly committees drafting a new Constitution for the Sudan, nodded his head in agreement.

One of the secrets of the new relationship lay in President Nimery's far-sighted decision to give top jobs to his bitterest opponents of the past. So I found, for example, Joseph Oduho, now a member of the twenty-five-strong National Political Bureau (with Cabinet rank) telling me that there was no dissension in the Bureau between Northerners and Southerners.

On National Unity Day—the first anniversary of the peace —the assassination of three Western diplomats brought indignation and embarrassment to the Sudanese nation. And in the same month a former brigadier of the Sudanese army stood trial on charges of having plotted to assassinate the President.

But Lagu had told me in Juba: 'If anyone tries to harm President Nimery he will have us—me—to deal with.'

After a year of peace I found the South still facing great difficulties born of the long and destructive war. Transportation, particularly in the South, was woefully inadequate. Again and again I heard of basic projects being held up through delays in getting vital materials. There were allegations of mistakes in planning, and of sabotage. Perhaps integration of the South was being pushed too quickly.

But these difficulties and inadequacies were inevitable.

The story now, I felt, was the story of a soldier turned states-man who was striving to lead his long-troubled country on to a new road of peace, stability and unity.

Let me conclude with a little incident which illustrated both the problems and the new attitudes. It was not possible to find good jobs for all former *Anya-Nyas*; and some of them, in common with the hundreds of thousands of displaced persons and returnees in the South, had to go through a trying transitional period. At a village called Nangala, about twenty miles from Juba, I talked with an *Anya-Nya* man, one of 173 who had to take jobs on the land and who said they had not been paid for three months and while waiting for their harvest had to sell their clothes for food. 'Are you angry?' I asked the man. 'Angry? No. Hungry? Yes,' he replied.

Appendix : Profiles

The pace of life in the Sudan may seem slow to the visitor, there is nothing static about the nation. Sudanese politics are so volatile that men who are at the time of writing virtually unknown to the outside world could be among those guiding the country's destiny tomorrow, and some of those who seem most significant today could be out of the picture.

But whatever the future may hold for him, **Gaafer Mohamed Nimery** will long be remembered for his key role in the drama of Sudan's war and peace. He was relatively little known, tried or tested as a leader when the military coup of 25 May 1969 swept him into power—although he had led a successful attack on the *Anya-Nya's* seemingly impregnable Deto Mountain defences in 1967. Six feet tall, President Nimery, born in 1930, graduated from the Sudan Military College as a second lieutenant in 1952; took a troop leader's course in Western Germany and a Master's Degree in Military Sciences in the United States; became Officer Commanding the infantry school, as a colonel, at Gebeit, near Port Sudan. Named President of the Revolutionary Command Council and promoted Major-General in 1969, Nimery was widely regarded as a bluff, energetic soldier. His stature grew and his personality mellowed with power. He was soon to be recognised as one of the most accessible and open leaders on the continent of Africa, with a leader's gift for inspiring loyalty. In September 1971 he showed popular support by his foregone success in a national referendum which confirmed him as President of Sudan. He made enemies as well as friends, and

160

for a while Southern supporters of the rebels regarded him as one of the worst of their oppressors. But after he had smashed the Communist coup of July 1971 and returned to power, more and more Southerners agreed that he was the first Northern leader who was keeping his promises to the South. In the post-war period his personal popularity in the South made him the recognised leader of the whole country.

Major-General Joseph Lagu, a devoutly religious, mission-taught Protestant, became the key man in the Southern Sudan (in war rather than in the immediate post-war period) as decisively as Major-General Nimery had become the key man in the North. Both men went to the same military college but although they are contemporaries, Lagu entered six years after Nimery graduated. They were in the same barracks at Juba in 1960. Both men have more than a touch of the quality known as charisma. Lagu, of medium height and slightly built, is sensitive, intelligent, cultured and (in conversation) soft-spoken—completely unlike the stereotyped image of a guerrilla leader. But I have heard warrior giants under his command refer to him reverently as 'The Leader'. A member of one of the smaller Southern Sudanese tribes, the Madi, he lived a simple, almost spartan, life. Anti-Communist and with a strong personal belief in Western democracy—which he told me he believed could work in Africa—he is too direct to feel at home in the sophisticated world of politics. He looks like a schoolmaster and he told me (on the eve of the Addis peace talks) that he would have rather been a school teacher than a soldier. He joined and became leader of the *Anya-Nya* because, in his own words, 'as a young man I realised that the only hope for my people in the South was to learn to fight back against the Northern oppressors'. He proved to be a born military strategist and tactician and, as fate would have it, he was given a post in the Sudan Defence Force with general's rank after he signed the peace treaty.

When Nimery overthrew the last of a series of party political governments in 1969 there passed from the active political

L

scene a man who in many ways was regarded as the personification of Northern Arab Sudanese conservatism. **Mohamed
Ahmad Mahgoub** had been at the centre of power more frequently than perhaps any other Sudanese politician since Independence. Born in 1908, a civil engineer and lawyer and
member of the *Ansar,* Mahgoub was Foreign Minister in the
UMMA-dominated coalition government of 1956 and held
office until the Abboud military coup of 1958. After Abboud
was ousted in 1964, Mahgoub resumed his post as Foreign
Minister until he became Prime Minister in 1965. In June
1966 he was replaced by Sadiq el-Mahdi but returned as
Prime Minister in May 1967 and stayed in power (heading
two governments) until a second military regime (Nimery's)
toppled him. Because of his ill-health (diabetes and a heart
complaint) he has since been living in semi-retirement in the
West End of London. He believed in a 'firm hand' against
rebels and, according to some Southerners, was noted during
his periods of power for his antipathy to the South. Alert,
dignified and conscious of his dignity, he is also a poet of
some renown. Every inch the aristocrat, he had a mother who
was, reputedly, a slave.

As was made clear in an earlier preceding chapter, **Sadiq
el-Mahdi**, after being exiled by General Nimery's government,
remained a significant actor in the wings in the Sudan drama.
Still in his thirties, he also remained something of an enigma.
This Oxford-educated, Western-looking great-grandson of
the original Mahdi is intelligent, modern-minded and has
great charm. But to many leading Southerners he was not a
man to depend on. They remembered that during his brief
rule his attitude to the South oscillated between 'high-
handedness' and readiness to compromise.

The man at one time regarded as the most formidable of
the Nimery government's political opponents was **Hussein
Sharif Yusif al-Hindi**. When the May 1969 coup took place,
Hindi—then Minister of Finance and Economy in the Mah-
goub government—went to Aba Island where he and the
Imam formed the nucleus of an opposition although al-Hindi

was not a member of the *Ansar* sect or of UMMA. In July 1969 while on a mission to Ethiopia for the Imam, Hindi sought political asylum and was granted temporary refuge. Hindi was accused of 'master-minding' an alleged plot by the Imam to overthrow Nimery in April 1970. After the Imam was killed in the Sudan government attack on Aba Island, Hindi reportedly joined forces with the Muslim Brotherhood (with whom previously he had little in common). The son of a wealthy Arab livestock trader and a leader of the Hindi religious sect. Sharif al-Hindi, at the age of 40, became Minister of Irrigation and Electric Power in Mohamed Mahgoub's first Cabinet in June 1965. He got the Finance and Economy post in 1967. His handling of it in a worsening economy was the subject of controversy, but he was generally respected in the North. The Nimery government at one time had little doubt that Hindi would strike against it when he could and with whom and what he could —if he could. But as Nimery's star rose, the danger from Hindi in exile receded. After the Addis agreement, Nimery, as part of his general policy of seeking reconciliation with former enemies, had a personal meeting with Hindi at Jiddah (Saudi Arabia). It was reported to be cordial and encouraged hopes of a new relationship.

The man chosen as President Nimery's deputy had resigned (in 1967) as Chief Justice of the Sudan because he opposed the then government's attempt to declare the Communist Party illegal. Although not a member of the Sudan Communist Party, **Babikir Awadalla** was a pro-Marxist. Presiding over the judiciary, he declared a civil strike against the Abboud regime in October 1964. He was appointed Premier and Foreign Minister after the May 1969 Revolution and became Deputy President of the Revolutionary Command Council. In October 1969 he was dropped from the Premiership after he had declared in an address to students in East Berlin that the Communist Party was the sole prop to the Sudanese regime. But he continued as Deputy President of the RCC and Minister of Justice. On 13 October 1971 he was appointed First Vice-President of the Sudan. But as the government became less and less receptive to Marxist ideas, his influence diminished, and in a reshuffle in the spring of 1972 he ceased to perform the functions of Vice-President.

Mystery surrounded the decision of Major-General **Khalid Hassan Abbas** in February 1972 to relieve himself of his duties as Minister of Defence. Abbas was reported to have opposed the peace negotiations with Southerners, and *Time* magazine (13 March 1972) said bluntly that President Nimery had dismissed him. Abbas, an army friend of Nimery and co-actor in the May coup, was only 33 when he was appointed Chief of Staff of the armed force in August 1969. Two months later he became Minister of Defence and on 13 October 1971 became a Vice-President. Known for his extreme pro-Egyptian views, General Abbas was treated like a Head of State when he visited Cairo shortly after relinquishing office.

Among ministers thought likely to play an increasing role in the 'new' Sudan were:

Mansour Khalid, who studied law in the United States, Europe and the Sudan, was visiting professor at Colorado University, President of the Arab Relations Section of UNESCO, Minister of Youth and Sport in June 1969, Permanent Representative of Sudan at the United Nations in 1970, and Minister for Foreign Affairs in October 1971 at the age of 40; **Omar El Hag Mousa**, a former soldier (brigadier) known for his intellect, appointed Minister of Defence in June 1969, Minister of National Guidance in October 1969 and, in 1971, Minister of Information and Culture. In the last job he had the important responsibility of improving Sudan's image in the outside world.

When regional self-government was obtained for the South under the Addis agreement, the man selected by President Nimery as President of the High Executive Council of the South was the distinguished Southerner, **Abel Alier**. A Dinka, born in Bor, Upper Nile Province, in 1933, Abel Alier Wal Kwai was one of the first Southerners to enter the Law Faculty of the University of Khartoum, receiving his LL.B degree in 1959 and his Master's degree at Yale in 1964. After serving as a judge, he resigned in 1965 to be one of the South's representatives at the Round Table Conference. He was Secretary-General of the Southern Front at the time of its dissolution and had represented Bor South in the Constituent Assembly. Appointed to the Nimery government in May 1969, as Minister of Housing, he became Minister of Supply in September of that year and Minister of Works in 1970. When, after Joseph Garang's execution, Alier was appointed Minister of State for Southern Affairs in August 1971 most Southerners were relieved. Unlike his predecessor, Alier is a man many Southerners trust (although some Liberation Front leaders took the view at the time that any Southerner who co-operated with the North was a 'collaborator'). Mr Alier evidently won President Nimery's trust and respect and on 13 October 1971 was appointed a Deputy President of the Republic while retaining his Southern Affairs portfolio. Noted for his powers of reasoning and his reasonableness, Abel Alier has always had the interest of the South at heart. He tends to be moderate in all matters. He is an Anglican.

The Southerner respected in the South perhaps above all others is **Clement Mboro**. A member of one of the smallest tribes of Bahr el Ghazal, the Ndogo, Clement Kutia Mboro had more than a quarter of a century in public life, having been one of the participants in the 1947 Juba Conference. He was Deputy Governor of Darfur Province when he became Minister of the Interior in the Caretaker Government of 1964. The Southerners' choice, he continued, as Minister, to be the champion of their cause. In 1965 he was elected President of the Southern Front. In the last elections before the 1969 military coup Clement defeated Joseph Garang so badly that Garang lost his deposit. Garang got the Ministry for Southern Affairs and his rival, Mboro, got a sentence of four years' imprisonment in 1970 on a political charge. His release a year later was a sign of a more conciliatory attitude by Khartoum to the South. An elder statesman, Clement, in his fifties, remained the acknowledged leader of the South. He was put in charge of resettlement.

Another Southern political leader to be arrested by the Nimery regime was **Hilary Paul Logali**. A contemporary of Clement Mboro, Hilary Logali is a Bari. A graduate of Khartoum University, he was at Yale University when in 1964 he was recalled to become Minister of Works and later Communications. He became Secretary-General of the Southern Front party and later its Vice-President. After one year's detention, he was released in 1970 and appointed one of the directors of the nationalised distilleries. In September 1971 he was appointed Commissioner of Equatoria Province. An obvious choice for the Executive Council of 1972. Intelligent, astute, respected in Equatoria. A Protestant.

The Commissioners for the other two Southern provinces were: Upper Nile: **Luigi Adwok**. Born in 1929, son of a Shilluk chief, he was a schoolteacher; became a member of the Constituent Assembly in 1958; member of Supreme Council of State from December 1964 to June 1965, Southern Minister of Education in 1972; and **Toby Madout**, born in Bahr el Ghazal Province (1939), of which he was to become Commissioner in October 1971, two months after he had been appointed a Minister of State.

Southern representation in the peace negotiations was on a wide basis and Southerners were anxious that the men chosen to run the South's affairs on a regional level in the post-war period should be no less representative. Among those most prominently involved were: the veteran Southern politician, **Ezbon Mondiri**, who, in the days of strife, could claim with many others to have 'graduated' for political honours by serving as a political prisoner. In his case it was a seven-year sentence after Mondiri, a Federalist member of the Southern Bloc, had drafted a Federal Constitution on United States lines for presentation to the Constituent Assembly of 1958 and had tried to rally Northern politicians from underdeveloped areas to support the Southern demand. Along with Mboro and Logali, he was appointed a Minister (Communications) as a Southern nominee, in the 1964 Caretaker Government. Not long after he chose exile. During the rise of the *Anya-Nya* Liberation Front, Mondiri was temporarily out of the picture, but he was chief of the Southern delegation to the Addis peace talks in February 1972.

Joseph Oduho, a one-time President of the Sudan African National Union (SANU), and a former Assistant Secretary-General of the Liberal Party, and President of the Azania Liberation Front (ALF). Arrested, tried and sentenced to death in 1955 for his alleged role in the revolt, he was acquitted three days before the day fixed for his execution. A member of the short-lived Sudan Parliament of 1958, Oduho fled to Uganda in 1960 where he continued his campaign for the Southern cause. After eclipse of SANU and ALF, Oduho was in the background but in the post-war period became a member of the National Political Bureau, and was responsible for housing in the South;

Mading de Garang, one-time Presbyterian church secretary, who established and edited *Grass Curtain* and became *Anya-Nya* overall representative in Europe, with headquarters in London. Mading, 40, played a big part in the Addis peace negotiations where he was a leading spokesman for the *Anya-Nya*. He became Southern Minister of Information, Culture and Tourism;

Lawrence Wol Wol: a Dinka, like Mading de Garang, his close associate. The intellect of the Liberation Front, Wol Wol, graduate of Freiburg University and Bordeaux, presented PhD thesis in Political Science at Bordeaux—a comprehensive study of the Southern Sudan. A founder and editor of the *Voice of Southern Sudan,* he was a member of the SANU delegation at the Round Table Conference in 1965; detained in prison in 1966; became *Anya-Nya* emissary in France; was one of eight Southern Sudanese delegates at the Addis peace talks. A Catholic, in middle thirties, he obtained the high post of Minister of National Planning;

Fredrick Maggott, a former captain in the Sudanese Army, became No 3 to General Lagu in the *Anya-Nya*, as Commander of Equatoria Brigade. With Lawrence Wol Wol, presented petition to UN in New York. Was delegate at Addis talks. Protestant;

Elia Lupe, a member of the Kakwa tribe, was one of the first Southern police officers and became Chief Inspector. In 1957 became MP for Yei, his home town. A Protestant who commanded respect among refugees and *Anya-Nya*, he was appointed Chief Commissioner in Lagu's Liberation Movement and was expected to play important administrative role in post-war South. Age about fifty;

Job Adier, Dinka, former headmaster who became official representative of *Anya-Nya* in Ethiopia. Was shot in leg in Upper Nile province in 1970 and walks with limp. Delegate at Addis talks.

Other delegates at Addis included **Angelo Voga**, Anya-Nya representative in East Africa, highly respected for his sincerity; **Oliver Albino**, author of the informative book, *The Sudan: A Southern Viewpoint;* and **Paul Puet.**

Among other Liberation Movement leaders were **Colonel Emmanuel Abur (Nhial)**, a Dinka from Bahr el Ghazal, who at the age of thirty rose to be Commander of the Third Brigade of the *Anya-Nya* in General Lagu's High Command; **Elisapana Mulla**, whom General Lagu appointed Commissioner for Equatoria and won a high reputation for his administrative abilities; **Antipas Ayiei**, Commissioner for Upper Nile in the Liberation Movement; **Disham Ojwe**, Police Commissioner in the Movement and a former Chief Inspector of Police (member of the Acholi tribe), and **Dominic Mohamed**, the *Anya-Nya's* able emissary in Washington, who did much to acquaint the world press with the struggle in the Southern Sudan.

Odd man out in the peace settlement was **Gordon Muortat Mayen**, who was quick to denounce it. Mayen, a veteran Southern politician, was Minister of Works in the 1964 Caretaker Government and Vice-President of the Southern Front. He was Foreign Minister in the Southern Sudan Provisional Government of 1967 and President of the breakaway Nile Provisional Government. When the NPG was dissolved in

1970, Mayen refused to accept Lagu's leadership and declared
himself president of the so-called and little-known 'African
National Front'.

Question marks had to go against the name of **Aggrey Jaden**,
leader of the Southern Sudan Provisional Government who
at one time was acceptable to most Southerners but became
involved in a divisive personal power struggle: **Samuel
Abujohn**, Zande leader who was General Lagu's Deputy Commander-in-Chief of the *Anya-Nya* was dismissed in the second
half of 1971 for 'unco-operative activities', but became a
colonel in the Sudan army after the Addis agreement.

Three of the most significant men in the Southern Sudan
story were killed. They were:

Joseph Ukel Garang, a highly intelligent and able Jura lawyer, long-time member of the Sudanese Communist Party,
who became Minister of Supply in Nimery's government in
May 1969, and then the Sudan's first Minister of State for
Southern Affairs. A Communist first and a Southerner second,
he made many enemies in the South who did not, however,
under-rate him. He was executed for his part in the Communist coup.

William Deng (Nhial), who became heavily involved in political controversy because he spoke out in favour of some form of
accommodation with the North at a time when other Southern
leaders felt that militancy was the only right course—and
because he split the Sudanese African National Union (see
chapter 7). His murder in 1968 shocked the South, and he is
remembered as a Southern patriot.

Joseph Akwon, who joined the *Anya-Nya* as a simple soldier
and was soon to show such outstanding military gifts and
intelligence that he was appointed Commander of the Upper
Nile forces with the rank of Brigadier in his early thirties and
succeeded Abujohn as Deputy Commander-in-Chief. He was
killed in action in the closing stages of the war. His death
shocked Southern leaders and others who saw in him a man of
almost limitless potential.

One of the least attractive figures in the Sudan drama is the

German mercenary, **Rolf Steiner,** sentenced to life imprisonment in Khartoum after a lengthy trial in 1971. Steiner, a
former Hitler Youth member and Nazi stormtrooper, was
accused of directing guerrilla operations in Southern Sudan.
He was discredited by the *Anya-Nya* leadership, who denied
that he had ever trained, commanded or even collaborated
with their forces but said (in the *Grass Curtain*, October 1971)
that he was involved with 'a self-styled general and president
of the Anyidi Republic'. It was considered unlikely that he
would be made to sit out his sentence.

No gallery of personalities in the Sudan story would be
complete without Major **Salah Salim,** the 'Dancing Major', who
was not a Sudanese at all but the Egyptian Special Minister
for Sudan Affairs. During the campaign in the South for the
1953 elections, he toured the Southern provinces on behalf of
the pro-Egyptian National Unionist Party, addressing public
meetings and promising the Southerners forty posts as Governors, District Commissioners and Assistant District Commissioners when the British left. 'At these meetings the backwardness of the South and the nakedness of some tribes were
the main theme and were blamed on the British,' writes
Oliver Albino (in *The Sudan: A Southern Viewpoint*). 'At
Rumbek Major Salim tried to prove that the Egyptians had
historical and blood relations with the Dinka tribe. Attribut-
ing the difference in the colour of his skin to the climate, he
at one time took off his shirt and joined a Dinka dance.'

What of the ladies? Sudanese women have not played
prominent public roles in the South, which remains largely a
man's world, although as wives and mothers they have had
their part behind the scenes and have suffered and died with
their menfolk. In the South of tomorrow there may be new
opportunities for them. Northern Sudanese women—at least
in the towns—are already among the freest in the Arab world.
Although it is still not customary for Sudanese Arab women
to be seen in public with men other than their fiances and
members of their families, more and more women have taken
up careers—including the army. First Sudanese woman

Cabinet Minister is attractive Mrs **Napisa Ahmed el Amin**—
Deputy Minister of Youth, Sport and Social Affairs. One of
the founders of the former Sudan's Women's Union, she is a
leading light of the (Socialist) Union of Sudanese Women,
founded in June 1971. By December of that year, she told me,
'we already have a million members'.

Notes and References

CHAPTER ONE

1 Major-General Mohamed Abdul Gadir, then Chief of Staff of the Sudanese army, in an interview with the author in Khartoum, 22 December 1971

2 Mr Abel Alier, a Southerner, then Minister of Supply and Internal Trade and later Vice-President of the Sudan Republic and Minister of State for Southern Affairs, speaking at Kampala on 9 February 1970

3 Beshir, Mohamed Omer, *The Southern Sudan—Background to Conflict*, London, New York, 1968. Mr Beshir was also Secretary of the Round Table Conference of 1965 and Head of the African section in the Ministry of Foreign Affairs in the Nimery government

4 Mr Omar el Hag Mousa, Minister of Information, in an interview with the author, Khartoum, 23 December 1971

5 President Nimery, Omdurman, 2 March 1972

6 *Basic Facts about the Southern Provinces of the Sudan*, Central Office of Information, Khartoum, 1964, p8

7 Ibid, p9

8 Sanderson, G. N., *England, Europe and the Upper Nile*, Edinburgh, 1965, pp6–7

9 Gray, R., *A History of the Southern Sudan, 1839–1889*, Salisbury, 1961, p68

10 Ibid, p32

11 One who did was Dominic A. Mohamed, international president of the union of Southern students, in an interview in *Politiken* (Copenhagen), 24 February 1971, in which he went on to say: 'My mother was a slave. It was not so long ago that this sort of thing was still found'

12 Lawrence Wol Wol, a representative of the Southern Sudan Liberation Front, in a letter to *The Washington Post*, 16 February 1971. In 1972 he became National Minister of Planning

13 For instance, A. Toynbee. Foreword to Albino, Oliver, *The Sudan —A Southern Viewpoint*, 1970

172

14 *Basic Facts*
15 In a confidential memorandum, 25 January 1930, the British Civil Secretary, Mr H. A. MacMichael, set out the policy of the government of the Southern Sudan as being 'to build up a series of self-contained racial or tribal units with structure and organisation based, to whatever extent the requirements of equity and good government permit, upon indigenous customs, traditional usages and beliefs'. Measures taken to promote the policy included the control of immigrant traders from the North, the use of English and the discouragement of Arabic in the South. A letter from the Acting Governor-General of the Sudan to the High Commissioner in Cairo, No 89/ICI Khartoum, 4 August 1945, restated Southern policy as being 'to act upon the fact that the people of the Southern Sudan are distinctly African and Negroid, and that our obvious duty to them is therefore to push ahead as fast as we can with their economic and educational development on African and Negroid lines, and not upon the Middle Eastern and Arab lines of progress which are suitable for the Northern Sudan. It is only by economic and educational development that these people can be equipped to stand for themselves in the future, whether their future lot be eventually cast with the Northern Sudan, or with East Africa (or partly with each)...'
16 Al-Rahim, Muddathir Abd, *Imperialism and Nationalism in the Sudan*, Oxford, 1969, p8. He also mentions the alleged involvement of Israel and other foreign countries in Sudanese separatism
17 Gray, R., Introduction to Joseph Oduho and William Deng, *The Problem of the Southern Sudan*, 1963 (quoting Northern allegations)
18 Sir J. W. Robertson, British Civil Secretary, Khartoum, 10 December 1946, in a secret letter to the governors of Southern provinces and other senior British officials in the Sudan
19 Eprile, C. L., *Sudan—The Long War*, Institute for the Study of Conflict Ltd, London, March 1972. Four posts of assistant district commissioner, plus two of Mamur (district administrative officers)—a total of six
20 The political parties of Northern Sudan and the forces behind them are briefly discussed in chapter 10
21 Albino, op cit
22 *Anya-Nya* is the deadly snake poison which the Southern Sudanese rebels adopted as a symbolic name in 1963
23 See chapter 4
24 Albino, op cit
25 See chapter 10
26 See chapter 8
27 See chapter 12
28 See chapter 9

CHAPTER TWO

1 Entire populations were enumerated in only sixty-eight towns (with a total population of 854,000) and a sampling method was used to estimate the remainder of the country's population

2 *Population Growth and Manpower in the Sudan*, a joint study by the United Nations and the government of the Sudan, New York, 1964

3 'It was estimated in 1958 that only about one out of five births and deaths was registered'—Harvie, C. H., 'Vital Statistics in Sudan' in *The Population of Sudan* (First Population Census of Sudan, 1955–56, Report on the Sixth Annual Conference of the Philosophical Society, Khartoum, 1958), p80

4 George P. Murdock in *Africa: Its People and their Cultural History*, rejects the use of the term 'Nilo-Hamitic' and instead describes such people as Nilotes who reflect a strong Cushitic influence

5 Trimingham, J. S., *Islam in the Sudan*, 1949, p5

6 Including, in this context, tribes (but not sub-tribes) of more than 10,000 members

7 Evans-Pritchard, E. E., *The Nuer*, Oxford, 1949

8 Professor C. G. Seligman in his foreword to Evans-Pritchard, E. E. *Witchcraft, Oracles and Magic among the Azande*, Oxford, 1937

9 *Basic Facts*

10 Omdurman address, 3 March 1972. See chapter 5

11 By 1966 there were estimated to be 165,000 to 170,000 Protestants in the country—the majority in the North

12 *Report of the Commission of Inquiry into the Disturbances in the Southern Sudan during August, 1955*, Khartoum, 18 February 1956 p7. The figures given were: between 25,000 and 30,000 Protestants; 180,000 to 200,000 Roman Catholics; 22,500 to 23,000 Southern Muslims

13 Jim Hoagland, *The Washington Post*, 6 June 1971

14 Ibid, 7 June 1971

15 Frederik Schjander, *A-Magazinet*, weekly insert of *Aftenposten* Oslo, 24 April 1971

16 See chapter 9

17 *Economic and Financial Bulletin*, July–September 1970, No 3, Vol XI, issued by the Economic Department of the Bank of Sudan Khartoum

18 David Hirst, *The Guardian*, London, 30 September 1971

19 *The Five-Year Plan of Economic and Social Development of the Democratic Republic of the Sudan for the Period 1970–71 to 1974–75*, Vol 1, 'Major Trends of Development', Ministry of Planning Khartoum, 1970. Targets listed were: 'Increased agricultural production; creation of marketable livestock; increase in industrial production; introduction of new types of products; development of economic and social services, including education, culture and health; development of urban and rural power networks; securing

of a favourable balance of trade; increased freight and passenger haulage volume by all modes of public transport; expediting the work on water supply—particularly in rural areas; stimulation of private investment; striving for "full employment" '

20 See chapter 5, n33
21 The Gezira (Arabic for 'island') is the six million-acre clay plain between the White and Blue Nile. The Gezira is the economic backbone of the Sudan
22 Colin Legum, *The Observer*, London, 8 August 1971
23 Interview with author, London, 24 August 1971
24 The team was chaired by P. P. Howell, MA, of the Sudan Political Service
25 *Natural Resources and Development Potential in the Southern Provinces of the Sudan*. A preliminary report by the Southern Development Investigation Team, 1954, Sudan Government, 1955
26 Morrison, Godfrey, *The Southern Sudan and Eritrea*, Minority Rights Group Report No 5, London, 1971
27 This was only one of many such disappointments. See chapter 9
28 *The Washington Post*, 27 June 1971
29 Garang, Joseph, *Revolution in Action*, No 6 On Economics and Regional Autonomy, published by Public Relations Bureau, Ministry for Southern Affairs, Khartoum, 1970. Joseph Garang, who was executed following the anti-Communist purge in 1972, was then Minister of State for Southern Affairs

CHAPTER THREE

1 *Report of the Commission of Inquiry*, Khartoum
2 The telegram, alleged to have been written by the then Prime Minister, Sayed Ismail El Azhari, on or about the beginning of July 1955, but, in fact, the work of a Southern clerk in Juba, ran as follows: 'To all my administrators in the three Southern provinces: I have just signed a document for self-determination. Do not listen to the childish complaints of the Southerners. Persecute them, oppress them, ill-treat them according to my orders. Any administrator who fails to comply with my orders will be liable to prosecution. In three months' time all of you will come round and enjoy the work you have done.' The telegram, typed on government paper, sometimes with slight variations, was widely circulated through Equatoria. One Southern senior private (named Saturlino) in the Southern Corps at Torit changed 'to my administrators in the three Southern provinces' to 'to my Northern officers in the Southern Corps'. The commissioners' comment was that the telegram would have done little harm in a sophisticated or educated community but in a primitive and backward community such as Southern Sudan, it could and did create irreparable harm
3 *Report of the Commission of Inquiry*, p87

4 Ibid, p102
5 The Nubas—from Southern Kordofan province in Central Sudan—are famed for their fighting qualities; the Camel Corps, in particular, have a reputation for never being known to refuse action
6 *Report of the Commission of Inquiry*, p22
7 The *Haggana* is a command composed mainly of Nuba and soldiers from Central Kordofan province
8 *Report of the Commission of Inquiry*, p54
9 Ibid, p57
10 Ibid, p59
11 Ibid, p61
12 Ibid, p69
13 The report commented: 'Since the Southern Sudanese benefited very little from Sudanisation, they found little or no differences between conditions now and conditions previously; and independence for them was regarded as merely a change of masters. We feel that the Southern Sudanese by finding themselves holding secondary positions in the government of their country have a genuine grievance.' (Page 117 of report)
14 The commission also gave the geographical, historical and cultural differences between Northern and Southern Sudanese which are covered in chapter 1 of this book
15 *Report of the Commission of Inquiry*, p81
16 Ibid, p6
17 Ibid, pp122–4
18 *Resistance: The Story of Southern Sudan*, report issued by Information Service, *Anya-Nya* National Organisation, London, 1971
19 Beshir, op cit, p73

CHAPTER FOUR

1 Reported by Gordian Troeller and Claude Deffarge, for *Stern* magazine, Hamburg. Reproduced under title, 'Slaughter in Africa' by *Atlas* magazine, October 1967
2 *Tiempo*, Montevideo, 29 January 1971
3 Frederic Hunter, *Christian Science Monitor*, 14 January 1971
4 An American journalist, Allan Reed, wrote in the *Daily Orange* Syracuse (New York), on 30 April 1970: 'Recent census figures in the liberated acreas of the Nile Provisional Government obtained from Chiefs and Sub-Chiefs show over 125,000 persons killed by the Arabs from April 1966 to November 1968. The figure of those massacred from 1955–1966 show over 890,000, which makes a total of 1,015,000 killed since the beginning of the struggle.' These figures are higher than those in other reports and must be treated with reserve
5 In 1970, Hamid Ali Shash, then Commissioner for Equatoria province, was reported to have told the well-known American correspon-

dent, Lawrence Fellows, that the figure of 500,000 dead must be wrong. Asked how many deaths he estimated, he said: 'I don't know. How can anyone know?'

6 Heradstveit, Per Oyvind, *Sudan—An African Tragedy*, Oslo, 1970

7 *Grass Curtain* (quarterly journal of the Southern Sudan Association, London, and official organ of the Southern Sudan Liberation Front), Vol 1, No 3, December 1970; the *Church Times*, London, 4 September 1970; *The Observer*, London, 30 August 1970; *Tribune*, 11 September 1970; *La Croix*, 2 October 1970; *Crusade*, November 1970; *March of the Nation*, 30 January 1971; and *Aftenposten*

8 *The Observer*, London, 30 August 1970

9 *Sudan Informazioni Documenti*, Milan, 1970, gave what purported to be a copy of a handwritten list of people killed at Banja and statements by two of the survivors, 17-year-old Edina Yambi and 38-year-old Grace Kwaji (both of whom described, among other details, how a cripple who could not walk was allegedly shot in the leg)

10 *Nile Mirror*, 18 September 1970

11 *Grass Curtain*, December 1970

12 Interview with author, Khartoum, 22 December 1971

13 *Christian Science Monitor*, 14 January 1971

14 *Grass Curtain*, Vol 1, No 4, April 1971

15 Frederik Schjander (from Khartoum), *Aftenposten*, Oslo, 20 March 1971

16 *Times*, London, 19 October 1970

17 Eprile, op cit

18 Ibid

19 *Grass Curtain*, August 1970

20 See n12

21 Lawrence Fellows, 'The Unknown War in the Sudan', *New York* magazine, 22 September 1970

22 Yangu, Alexis Mbali, *The Nile Turns Red*, New York, 1966. Mr Yangu's own father is said to have lost his eyesight and to have died, following his release from prison, as a result of torture

23 Memorandum presented by the Sudan African Liberation Front (SALF) to the 3rd summit conference of the Organisation for African Unity, Accra, 21 October 1965

24 Albino, op cit, p44

25 Mr Abel Alier, the most important Southerner in Nimery's administration, described 'the long imprisonment of schoolboys who protested against the abolition of Sunday as a public holiday' as one of the South's grievances. Mr Alier was addressing the Makerere Student Guild Centre, Kampala, on 9 February 1970. The address was published as No 3, *A Revolution In Action*, Ministry for Southern Affairs, Khartoum, June 1970

26 Memorandum by Sudan African National Union (SANU)

27 Listed as Case No 26 in the SANU memo to the OAU commission for refugees (November 1964) and Case No 21 in the SALF memo to

M

the OAU (October 1964)

28 pp180 seq of the *Answer* to the *Black Book*

29 Letter from the Southern Front, PO Box 2140, Khartoum, 19 January 1965

30 According to Yangu, op cit, p123, the note was signed by Clement Mboro, Hiltary Logali (Minister of Communications), Gordon Muortat (Minister of Works) and others, in addition to Mr Bong

31 Godfrey Morrison, op cit, wrote that 'anything between 1,000 and 3,000 people lost their lives'. According to Albino, op cit, p61, an official police report put the number of deaths at 1,019 (London *Times*, letter from Peter Kilner, Khartoum, 27 November 1965), but other reports put the toll at probably more than 1,400

32 Albino, op cit, p61, and a report from the Sudan African Liberation Front office: 'The Black Massacre in Juba as told by Eye-witnesses 8 July 1965,' *Voice of Southern Sudan*, 2/1964–5

33 *Voice of Southern Sudan*, 2/1964–5

34 Allan Reed, *Daily Orange*, Syracuse, New York, 30 April 1970

35 *Southern Sudan Information Service*, 1967—news service issued in London by Southern Sudanese leaders in exile

36 *The Vigilant* (closed down in May 1969), 24 January 1967

37 *The Vigilant*, 1 March 1962, named twenty-two

38 Article in *El Hayam* daily, translated from the Arabic into English in *The Vigilant*, 17 January 1967

39 Albino, op cit

40 Not to be confused with the William Nhial, killed in 1966

41 Dr Deng was interviewed by Robert Stevens, Yale Professor of Law *Yale Reports*, 7 February 1971

42 Lagu, J., 'The Dynamics of Co-operation between the *Anya-Nya* and the People', *Grass Curtain*, Vol 1, No 4, April 1971, p6

43 *Tiempo*, Montevideo, 29 January 1971

44 King, K. J., 'Nationalism, Education and Imperialism in the Southern Sudan, 1920–70', *East Africa and the Nile Valley Seminars Paper XIV*, Department of History, University of Nairobi, quoting from three interviews with the Rev J. Lowrie Anderson, formerly head of the American Presbyterian Mission in the Sudan (January–February 1971)

45 Ibid

CHAPTER FIVE

1 Said, B. M., *The Sudan: Crossroads of Africa*, 1965, Epilogue, p155

2 Colin Legum, writing in the introduction to *The Sudan: Crossroads of Africa* by B. M. Said, says that Mr Said is 'frankly partisan. A Northerner, he refuses to accept the charge that his own people are blameworthy for all that has gone wrong.' (p9)

3 See chapter 1

4 Said, op cit, p151

5 Five years later, Professor Muddathir Abd Al-Rahim (former Head

of the Department of Political Science, University of Khartoum, and later Visiting Professor at Makerere University College, Kampala) wrote that Arabism was 'a basic attribute of the majority of the population of the Sudan'. For him, Arabism was not a racial bond but 'a cultural, linguistic and non-racial link' between a number of races. Culturally the Sudan was far more homogenous than it was racially. 'For although slightly more than one-third of the total population claim Arab descent, over half speak Arabic as their mother tongue, while most of the rest, including the Southern Sudanese, use Arabic, or a pidgin form of it, as a *lingua franca*.' This was because 'the majority of the Sudanese are Muslims and historically speaking the spread of Islam went hand in hand with that of the language of the Koran. Secondly, the fact that Arabic is the national language and that it is the language used in business, education, journalism, broadcasting and in government offices at once explains and propagates its adoption throughout the country.' *Imperialism and Nationalism in the Sudan*, pp5 and 7; and *The Journal of Modern African Studies*, 8(2), 1970, pp237 and 248

6 Said, op cit, pp152–3
7 Ibid, p150
8 Mr Said quotes Sir James Robertson as saying that he was not suggesting that the future of the inhabitants of the South should be influenced by appeasement of the politicians in the North. 'But it is the Sudanese, Northern and Southern, who will live their lives and direct their affairs in future generations in this country; and our efforts must therefore now be concentrated on initiating a policy ... which can be made acceptable to, and eventually workable by, patriotic and reasonable Sudanese, Northern and Southern alike.' Letter from J. W. Robertson, British Civil Secretary, 16 December 1946
9 Said, op cit, p46
10 See chapter 1
11 Said, op cit, p72
12 Ibid, p87
13 Ibid, p107
14 Ibid, p112
15 Ibid, p187
16 Ibid. Mr Said is quoting the opinion expressed by J. S. R. Duncan on p215 of his book, *The Sudan*
17 Ibid, p190
18 Ibid, p100 and p111
19 *Basic Facts*, p25
20 Ibid, p19
21 Ibid, p25
22 Beshir, op cit, p83
23 Ibid, p92
24 Albino, op cit, p58
25 Beshir, op cit, pp93, 96, 97

26 Mr Beshir's exact words were: 'The two incidents at Juba on 8 July 1965, and at Wau on 8 August 1965, where a number of Southerners were killed as a result of army and police activities against the rebels and their sympathisers, left behind them an increased bitterness . . .'
27 Ibid, p100
28 Ibid, p106
29 *Basic Facts*
30 Ibid, p48
31 Said, op cit
32 Beshir, op cit, p4
33 *The Five-Year Plan*, Vol 1
34 Mr Abel Alier
35 *The New Educational Policy*—official documents series, Ministry of Education, Khartoum, May 1970
36 Eprile, op cit, p7
37 Author's note: This should not be taken as more than a reporter's impression. One would have to live in the place, win the confidence of the ordinary people and speak their dialect to get the whole truth
38 According to *Time* magazine, 2 August 1971, p20, even the most hard-line Communist recognised the importance of the Muslim faith to the Northern Sudanese Arabs—by having verses of the Koran chanted in unison at Sudanese Communist Party meetings
39 Omdurman address, 3 March 1972

CHAPTER SIX

1 See chapter 3
2 *Report of the Commission of Inquiry* (Judge T. S. Cotran was Chairman)
3 King, op cit
4 *Basic Facts*, pp19–20
5 See n3
6 These figures, based on a memorandum from the Ministry of the Interior, Khartoum, 5 March 1964, which gave a detailed list of missionary personnel, specifying their numbers in each locality, were challenged by Catholic missionaries in Verona, who wrote: 'We are absolutely certain that the Catholic missionaries in Southern Sudan were at the moment of the general expulsion only 214, including some who were at the time in Europe on leave. And it may not be amiss to add that in Southern Sudan we have left, in this century, the graves of sixty-four missionaries.' *The Black Book of the Sudan: an Answer*, Verona, 5 August 1964
7 Beshir, op cit, p82
8 Ibid
9 *Basic Facts*, pp27 and 28
10 Said, op cit, p88
11 Duncan, J. S. R., *The Sudan*, London, 1952, pp217–18

12 Henderson, K. D. D., *The Making of the Modern Sudan: The Life and Letters of Sir Douglas Newbold*, London, 1953, p106

13 Ali Abdel Rahman

14 Southern Front memorandum to the Organisation of African Unity, Accra, October 1965

15 Sayed Ziada Osman Arabab, a Northerner, speaking in Parliament on 13 February 1957

16 Southern Front memorandum to the Organisation of African Unity, Accra, October 1965

17 As evidence of 'educational subjection' in the South, Oduho and Deng, op cit, pp45–8, wrote that 'prior to independence the South had a well-established education system' but since then there had been a 'failure of the Juba and Malakal schools, which have been run for years in Arabic, to bring a single African child beyond the intermediate level'

18 *Basic Facts*, p82

19 *The Black Book*

20 K. J. King (see n3), quoting from interviews with the Rev J. Lowrie Anderson, formerly head of the American Presbyterian Mission in the Sudan, January–February 1971

21 Said, op cit, pp107–8. See also chapter 5

22 The Cotran commission of inquiry into the disturbances in Southern Sudan during August 1955

23 *The Black Book*, p25

24 The missionaries quoted American news agency correspondent, Patrick O'Connor: 'Those who served formerly in the Sudan will perhaps see some humour in the theory that Italian Catholic missionaries could have been agents of the British regime'

25 Sayed Ziada Osman Arabab. See n15

26 Major-General Nasr Osman, *The Black Book*, p92, quoting *The Sudan Daily*, 28 February 1964

27 The book gives the text of documents written by the Governor-General, Sir Knox Helm (3 September 1955), by Colonel Hassan Beshir Nasr, then Commander Troops, Juba (5 September 1955) and by Prime Minister Ismail el Azhari (2 February 1956) 'proving that the missionaries saved the lives of more than eighty Northern Sudanese', pp92–4

28 For estimates of numbers see chapter 2

CHAPTER SEVEN

1 Albino, op cit, p29

2 Ibid, p38

3 Buth Diu was reported to have appealed to the mutineers to surrender

4 David Wm McClintock, in *The Middle East Journal* (Middle East Institute), Washington DC, 1970, quoting *Keesing's Contemporary*

Archives, 29 March–5 April 1958, p1609A. Mr McClintock describes the Bloc as the 'Federal Bloc', but nomenclatures in Southern Sudanese politics tended to vary. According to Yangu, op cit, p55, Father Saturnino was elected President-General of the Liberal Party. Yangu, who was Father Saturnino's private secretary and one-time Deputy Secretary-General of the Liberal Party, describes how before the 1958 elections Saturnino resigned as leader of a group of three Southern members of a Constitution Committee over failure to reach a compromise with the six Northern Arab members of the committee on a federal form of government

5 See Appendix. Mondiri was later to head the Southern delegation at the Addis peace talks in February 1972

6 See chapter 1

7 'The name *Azania* was that given to an East African civilisation of some 4,000 years ago, and is of only dubious relevance to the Sudan.' Albino, op cit, p59

8 Ibid, p57

9 Ibid

10 For profiles of these and other Southern leaders see Appendix

11 Details of some of these excesses are given in chapter 3

12 Albini, op cit, p37

13 George Hunter, *The Daily Express*, London, 16–17 March 1971

14 Tom Stacey, *The Daily Telegraph* magazine, 26 April 1968

15 David Robison, *The Observer*, London, 7 March 1971

16 See short profile of Steiner in Appendix

17 Eprile, op cit

18 Among commanders replaced were General Emilio Tafeng and Colonel Samuel Abujohn. The Southern Sudanese Provisional Government (SSPG) in 1967–8 had placed the *Anya-Nya* under nominal control (with its name changed to *Anya-Nya* National Armed Forces —ANAF), and the then military Commander-in-Chief, Tafeng, was made responsible to President Jaden. But the *Anya-Nya* forces of Eastern Equatoria, which had established its own command structure under the then Colonel Lagu, remained outside the SSPG jurisdiction. After the collapse of both the SSPG and Tafeng's 'Anidi government' both Tafeng and his No 2, Fredrick Maggott, joined Lagu in April 1970. Two months later Lagu engineered a coup against the Nile Provisional Government by their own Chief of Staff, Emmanuel Abur. When the western commander, Abujohn, also declared loyalty to Lagu, Lagu was able, by January 1971, to announce the formation of the Southern Sudan Liberation Front —with himself as Commander-in-Chief and Abujohn as Deputy C-in-C. Tafeng was put on pension and appeared to play no part in subsequent proceedings. In October that year General Lagu announced that he had dismissed Abujohn. According to *Grass Curtain*, Vol 2, No 3, October 1971, Abujohn had 'developed an uncooperative attitude to the Command, lacked seriousness for his work and had been accused of insubordination' (see Appendix). Other

Southern sources told the author that Abujohn had plotted to seize power from Lagu

19 Brigadier Akuon was killed just before the cessation of hostilities. See profile in Appendix

20 Lagu, op cit

CHAPTER EIGHT

1 Giving an example of the way the Russians had sought to influence Khartoum, ex-Premier Mahgoub told the author that when he signed his own arms deal with Russia, the Soviet Ambassador asked him to recognise East Germany as a gesture of goodwill. Mahgoub said he refused on the grounds that Sudan's independence in such matters was not negotiable. 'But one of the first things the Nimery regime did after the May takeover was to recognise East Germany'

2 Hoagland, Jim, *The Washington Post*, 17 June 1971, estimated 200; *Morgenbladet*, Oslo, 22 February, 1971, quoting Dominic A. Mohamed, international president of the Union of Southern Sudanese Students, estimated 3,000; *Swiss Review of World Affairs*, February 1971: 1,500 Soviet military instructors—and still growing; *Der Spiegel*, 15 March 1971: between 500 and 1,000 Russians were drilling Nimery's 30,000 soldiers; Warren Howe, Russell, *The Baltimore Sun*, 7 July 1971 (from Addis Ababa): more than 100 Russian intelligence staff members and about 1,000 field 'advisers', including gunship pilots, had reportedly been brought into the Sudanese forces under two key Soviet defence advisers, named Youry Moukhine and Pavel Poliakov; Robison, David, *The Observer*, London, 7 March 1971, said that a western teacher in Omdurman last summer had told him of hearing Soviet army instructors giving orders to Sudan troops—in Russian

3 Fischler, Stan, *The Toronto Daily Star*, 4 January 1971, quoted the sources. They were corroborated by Evans, Rowland and Novak, Robert, *The Washington Post*, 1 January 1971

4 Robison, David, *The Observer*, London, 7 March 1971

5 John Chadwick, in a *Reuter* report from Khartoum (13 June 1971) said: This year, on the second birthday of General Nimery's army-backed revolution, the Russians put on their biggest military show yet. 'Even Nimery ducked as a flight of precision-flown Mig jets with Soviet pilots at the controls screamed at little more than tree-top height across the River Nile. Sudanese commandos dropped into the river from Russian helicopters and in a mock exercise stormed an island in mid-river with Soviet weapons. And Sam-2 missiles were on show for the first time in Sudan'

6 Chimelli, Rudolph, *Süddeutsche Zeitung*, 22 January 1971

7 *Morgenbladet*, Oslo, 26 January 1971

8 *Der Spiegel*, 15 March 1971

9 *Grass Curtain*—quarterly bulletin published from London under

the auspices of the Southern Sudan Association

10 A London report, published on 10 January 1971, by *Eleftheros Kosmos* (of Athens) said that 'about sixty Mig-21 Soviet planes, mostly operated by Soviets, are stationed in Juba'. Fairhall, John, *The Guardian*, Manchester, 5 March 1971, spoke of thirty Mig-17s and Russian-built bombers and helicopters being used

11 Sager, Peter, *Swiss Press Review and News Report*, Berne, 26 April 1971

12 Robison, David, *The Observer*, London, 7 March 1971

13 Bartlett, Charles, *The Chicago Sunday Times*, 30 December 1970

14 Sylvester, Anthony, *The Daily Telegraph*, London, 22 June 1971

15 Hoagland, Jim, *The Washington Post*, 27 June 1971

16 Robison, David, *The Sunday Star*, Washington, 4 April 1971

17 Published in *The Zambia Daily Mail*, 5 April 1971

18 Fairhall, John, *The Guardian*, Manchester, 5 March 1971

19 Mr Odeyo Owiti Ayaga, Assistant Professor, African Studies Programme and Political Science Department, Howard University, Philadelphia, on behalf of the Afro–Asian Institute. His letter was published in *The Washington Post*, 12 January 1971

20 Evans, Rowland and Novak, Robert, *The Washington Post*, 1 January 1971

21 *The Sunday Post*, Lagos, Nigeria, 6 June 1971

22 Letter in *New Times*, USSR, 24 March 1971

23 *Swiss Review of World Affairs*, February 1971, reported that Yugoslavia was constructing a naval academy in the Port Sudan area

24 *Der Spiegel*, 15 March 1971; *Swiss Press Review and News Report*, Berne, 26 April 1971. And the *Daily Nation*, Nairobi, 16 June 1971, said that the Sam-2 missiles 'were presumably detected by US electronic surveillance since American Air Force sources state that the presence of the Russian missiles at Port Sudan is a certainty'

CHAPTER NINE

1 Legum, Colin, *The Observer*, London, 8 August 1971

2 Tickle, Ian, *Swiss Press Review and News Report*, Berne, 10 May 1971

3 After the assassination of Major-General Sir Lee Stack, Governor-General of the Sudan, on 19 November 1922, Lord Allenby, British High Commissioner in Egypt, delivered a strongly-worded ultimatum to the Egyptian government, requiring them, among other things, to 'order within twenty-four hours the withdrawal from the Sudan of all Egyptian officers and the purely Egyptian units of the Egyptian army' and to note that 'the Sudan government will increase the area to be irrigated in the Gezira from 300,000 feddans to an unlimited figure. . .' Muddathir Abd Al-Rahim, op cit, p107; Marlowe, J., *Anglo–Egyptian Relations 1800–1953*, London, 1954, pp268–9; K. D. D. Henderson, op cit, p63

4 Redan, Edith, 'Russia's Thin End of the Wedge', Forum World Features, 8 January 1972
5 *Newsweek*, 18 January 1971
6 See previous chapter
7 With Legum, Colin, *The Observer*, London, 1 August 1971
8 Hoagland, Jim, *The Washington Post*, 27 May 1971
9 Johns, Richard, *The Financial Times*, London, 21 July 1971
10 Lavrencic, Karl, *The Daily Telegraph*, London, 2 September 1971
11 Hirst, David, *The Guardian*, Manchester, 30 September 1971. (The minister in question was unnamed)
12 Ibid
13 Eprile, op cit
14 The team who published the book in Moscow in March 1971 was headed by V. G. Solodovnikov, Director of the African Institute of the USSR Academy of Sciences
15 Eric Rouleau in *Le Monde*, Paris, 18 February 1972, said that while President Nimery in August 1971 'told us he had no proof whatever of any Soviet participation in the July coup, he now states categorically that the Kremlin was perfectly aware of the plot and supported it from the start'. As evidence President Nimery was quoted as saying: 'From 26 June to the day of the *putsch* Moscow refused to grant a visa to General Abbas, the Defence Minister, and to the members of the delegation which intended to discuss some important matters in the Soviet capital'
16 Ul'yanovski, R. A., 'Marxists and non-Marxist Socialism', *World Marxist Review*, No 9, 1971, p41
17 Ponomarev, B., 'Current problems of the theory of the World Revolutionary Process', *Kommunist*, No 15, 1971, pp62–71
18 *Al Ahram*, 5 August 1971
19 Farouk Nassar of Associated Press in Beirut, 2 March 1972
20 The Chinese, who had been quoting Soviet participation in an 'Arab–African war' in Southern Sudan as evidence of Russia's 'racial prejudice', switched their propaganda and took the opportunity of exploiting the Khartoum–Moscow controversy by assuring the Sudan of China's support in preserving Sudanese independence 'against all pressures'. President Nimery requested the Chinese to send more technicians to the Sudan; and early in August 1971, General Khalid Hassan Abbas, then Minister of Defence, left for China, accompanied by Mr Mansour Mahgoub, Minister of Economy, and Col Muhammad Abdul Halim, Minister of Finance and Planning, on a mission to strengthen relations between Khartoum and Peking. Moscow reacted by accusing the Chinese of being 'eloquently silent' on the 'bloody terror' in the Sudan (*Tass*, 30 July) and of even welcoming 'those whose hands were stained with the blood of Sudanese Communists and Democrats' (broadcast in Arabic, 4 August 1971). Moscow was still hammering on this theme as late as 21 December 1971, when a *Tass* message claimed that a further visit to Peking by a Sudanese government delegation, again led by General Abbas

(16–20 December 1971), proved 'collusion' between China and Khartoum. *Tass* quoted *The Washington Post* as describing the Abbas visit to China as 'a step towards *rapprochement* between Peking and Khartoum after Nimery adopted an anti-Soviet stand'

21 Interview with Farouk Nassar, Associated Press, Beirut, Lebanon, 2 March 1972
22 Agence France-Presse, Abu Dhabi, Persian Gulf Emirate, 2 March 1972

CHAPTER TEN

1 Jim Hoagland, *The Washington Post*, 30 May 1971
2 *The Times*, London, 29 July 1971
3 October issue, 1971, Vol 2, No 2, p13
4 Stanley Meisler, *International Herald Tribune*, 27 September 1971
5 *The Times*, London, 20 July 1971
6 First, Ruth, 'Sudan—Behind the Coups', *Africa* monthly, No 3, 1971, pp60–62
7 *Le Monde* weekly, 17 February 1971
8 According to David Robison in 'War on the Nile', *The Observer*, London, 7 March 1971
9 Mohamed Mahgoub, former Prime Minister of the Sudan, in an interview with the author, London, January 1972
10 See chapter 1 for details
11 *Le Monde* weekly, 17 February 1971
12 See n9
13 Jim Hoagland, *The Guardian*, Manchester, 27 May 1971
14 Interview with author in East Africa, December 1971

CHAPTER ELEVEN

1 *Der Spiegel*, Hamburg 15 March 1971
2 Confirmed to the author by Mr Ashour Frtas, Acting Director of the Political Department of the Libyan Ministery of Unity and Foreign Affairs in Tripoli, 20 October 1971
3 *The New York Times*, 23 May 1972
4 Ibid, 18 April 1971
5 Anthony Nutting of the London *Times*, quoted in *Atlas*, February 1971
6 *Tass*, 18 March 1971
7 Reported in the *Nigerian Observer*, 12 March 1971; *Time* magazine, 1 March 1971; *The Observer*, London, 7 March 1971; *Der Spiegel*, 15 March 1971. But John Fairhall in the *The Guardian*, Manchester, 5 March 1971, while saying: 'No wonder the Israelis are providing support for the *Anya-Nya*' added: 'I have no evi-

dence to support the allegation that Israeli arms are being air-dropped'

8 David Robison, *The Observer*, London, 7 March 1971

9 *Morgenbladet*, Oslo, 26 January 1971

10 See Appendix

11 These terms were used in an appeal—*The Southern Front Memorandum to OAU* on Afro-Arab conflict in the Sudan, Accra, October 1965—sent from Khartoum and signed by Clement Mboro, Southern Front President; Gordon Muortat, Vice-President; Hilary Paul N. Logali, Secretary-General; Luigi A. Bong; Abel Alier

12 *Time* magazine, 13 March 1972

13 *The New York Times*, 27 February 1972

14 Omdurman Radio Domestic Service in Arabic, 27 February 1971

15 Ibid

16 *The People*, Kampala, 27 January 1972

17 Events behind the peace negotiations are discussed in the next chapter

18 Brian MacDermot, chairman of the South Sudan Association, London, reported in March 1971, after a visit to Ethiopia, Kenya and Uganda, that, counting unregistered refugees, the total number of refugees probably exceeded 250,000 (*Grass Curtain*, Vol 1, No 4, April 1971.) A prominent church leader, in a private conversation with me, agreed that the total was over a quarter of a million, including those refugees not in camps who had assimilated into African populations. Later in 1971, Godfrey Morison, Editor of *Africa Confidential*, estimated (in his paper, *The Southern Sudan and Eritrea*) that there were about 20,000 Southern Sudanese refugees in Ethiopia, an estimated 178,000 in Uganda, about 66,000 in the Congo and about 22,000 in the Central African Republic. Another report in the *Grass Curtain*, Vol 1, No 4, April 1971, put the number of refugees at between 350,000 and 400,000, plus 50,000 to 100,000 'seasonal refugees'

CHAPTER TWELVE

1 Beshir, op cit, Appendix 17, p179. According Albino, op cit, p55, a fourth choice—regional government—was envisaged in the suggested plebiscite, but this is not included in Mr Beshir's record

2 Beshir, op cit, p95

3 One responsible Southerner told the author that in the view of many colleagues and himself, there had been no logic in Britain's decision to declare the Northern and Southern Sudan one geographical enitity in the first place but it was too late to change now and for economic reasons co-existence within a unified Sudan was the only practicable answer

4 *The Observer*, London

5 *The New York Post*, 15 April 1971

6 *Grass Curtain*, Vol 2, No 2, October 1971, p3
7 The Sudanese delegation to Scandinavia comprised Abel Alier (then Minister of Works), Abdeen Ismail Hussein(then Ambassador to the United Kingdom), Mohamed Omer Beshir (then Ambassador, Head of African Section, Ministry of Foreign Affairs), Abdel Rahman El Beshir (Director, Ministry of Interior, Refugee Affairs), Ahmed El Tayeb (Ministry of National Guidance, Director of Television), Numan Khogali (Chief of Protocol, Ministry of Foreign Affairs), Othwonh Dak (Director of Information, Ministry of Southern Affairs), Osman El Sayed Fadleiseed (Secretary to the Council of Ministers) and Philip Obang (then Counsellor, Embassy of Sudan, United Kingdom)
8 Vice-President Abel Alier at a press conference in Sudan, 7 March 1972
9 *Morgenbladet,* report by Gunnar Moe, quoting Theofilio Occang-Loti, a representative of the SSLF, at a press reception in Oslo, 27 April 1971
10 See profile in Appendix
11 A copy of the draft was given to the author at the time
12 See chapter 7 and Appendix
13 See profiles, Appendix
14 *Time* magazine, 13 March 1972, p40
15 President Nimery, Omdurman, 3 March 1972
16 *The New York Times*, 24 March 1972
17 See profile, Appendix
18 Agence France Presse, Kinshasa, 27 February 1972
19 A copy of the amended draft came into the author's possession
20 Eprile, C. L., 'Tricky Issues in Sudan Peace', Forum World Features, 25 March 1972

Bibliography

Albino, Oliver, *The Sudan—A Southern Viewpoint*, 1970

Al-Rahim, Muddathir Abd, *Imperialism and Nationalism in the Sudan*, Oxford, 1969

Bank of Sudan, *Economic and Financial Bulletin*, July–September 1970; No 3, Vol XI

Basic Facts about the Southern Provinces of the Sudan, Central Office of Information, Khartoum, 1964

Beshir, Mohamed Omer, *The Southern Sudan: Background to Conflict*, London, 1968

The Black Book of the Sudan: an Answer, Verona, 5 August 1964

Duncan, J. S. R., *The Sudan*, 1952

Eprile, C. L., *Sudan—The Long War*, Institute for the Study of Conflict, London, March 1972

Evans-Pritchard, E. E., *The Nuer*, Oxford, 1949
—*Witchcraft, Oracles and Magic among the Azande*, Oxford 1937

First, Ruth, 'Sudan—Behind the Coups', *Africa Monthly*, No 3, 1971

Five Year Plan of Economic and Social Development of the Democratic Republic of the Sudan for the period 1971–72 to 1974–75, Vol 1, 'Major Trends of Development', Ministry of Planning, Khartoum, 1970

Garang, Joseph, *Revolution in Action*, No 6, Public Relations Bureau, Ministry of Southern Affairs, Khatoum, 1970

Gray, R., *A History of the Southern Sudan, 1839–1899*, Salisbury, 1961

Henderson, K. D. D., *The Making of the Modern Sudan*, 1953

Heradstveit, Pet Oyvind, *Sudan—An African Tragedy*, Oslo, 1970

King, K. J., Nationalism, Education and Imperialism in the

Southern Sudan, 1920-70. *East African and the Nile Valley Seminars*, Paper XIV, Department of History, University of Nairobi

Morrison, Geoffrey, *The Southern Sudan and Eritrea*, Minority Rights Group Report, No 5, London, 1971

Murdock, G. P., *Africa: Its People and their Cultural History*, New York, 1959

Lagu, J., 'The Dynamics of Co-operation between the *Anya-Nya* and the People, *Grass Curtain*, Vol 1, No 4, April 1971

Natural Resources and Development Potential in the Southern Provinces of the Sudan, Sudan Government, 1955

The New Educational Policy—official documents series, Ministry of Education, Khartoum, May 1970

Oduho, Joseph and William Deng, *The Problem of the Southern Sudan*, 1963

Ponomarev, B., 'Current problems of the theory of the World Revolutionary Process', *Kommunist*, No 15, 1971

Report of the Commission into the Disturbances in the Southern Sudan during August 1955, Khartoum, 18 February 1956

Resistance: The Story of the Southern Sudan, Information Service, *Anya-Nya* National Organisation, 1971

Said, B. M. *The Sudan: Crossroads of Africa*, 1965

Sanderson, G. N., *England, Europe and the Upper Nile*, Edinburgh, 1965

Trimmingham, J. S., *Islam in the Sudan*, 1949

Ul'yanovski, R. A., 'Marxists and no-Marxist Socialism', *World Marxist Review*, No 9, 1971

United Nations and the Government of the Sudan, *Population and Manpower in the Sudan*, New York, 1964

Yangu, Alexis Mbali, *The Nile Turns Red*, New York, 1966

Index

191